1 For Your Information

Reading and Vocabulary Skills

Second Edition

KAREN BLANCHARD   CHRISTINE ROOT

PEARSON
Longman

For Your Information 1, Second Edition

Pearson Education, 10 Bank Street, White Plains, NY 10606

Staff credits: The people who made up the *For Your Information 1* team, representing editorial, production, design, and manufacturing, are: Rhea Banker, Aerin Csigay, Mindy DePalma, Christine Edmonds, Laura Le Dréan, Linda Moser, Edith Pullman, Mykan White, and Pat Wosczyk.
Cover design: MADA Design, Inc.
Text composition: TexTech International Pvt Ltd
Text font: 11/14 New Aster
Illustrator credits: Donna M. DeLuca for TSI Graphics, Inc. 113, 139; Jill Wood pp. 3, 69, 116, 157
Photo credits: p. 1 Mitch Diamond/Index Stock Imagery; p. 3 (left) www.bikeforbreath.org, (right) www.bikeforbreath.org; p. 9 Arto/Fotolia; p. 14 Copyright © 2001 Bob Sacha; p. 21 LLC, Vstock/Index Stock Imagery; p. 24 (left) www.ilovepeanutbutter.com, (right) Photo courtesy of Mykan White; p. 30 Photo courtesy of Alan Bressler; p. 34 Elizabeth Simpson/Getty Images; p. 36 Alt-6/Alamy; p. 45 © 2006 Mick Stevens from cartoonbank.com. All rights reserved; p. 59 www.techshout.com; p. 67 (left) LWA-Dann Tardif/Corbis, (right) Royalty-Free/Corbis, (bottom) AbleStock/Index Stock Imagery; p. 69 Photo courtesy of Lisa Cohen; p. 75 Photo courtesy of A.J. La Fleur; p. 81 © 1998 Randy Glasbergen. www.glasbergen.com; p. 91 (left) Tim Pannell/Corbis, (right) Tim Pannell/Corbis, (bottom) Turbo/zefa/Corbis; p. 100 www.sejongkorean.org; p. 105 North Wind Picture Archives/Alamy; p. 111 Tim Davis/Corbis; p. 113 Republished with permission of Globe Newspaper Company, Inc., from the May 10, 2000 issue of *The Boston Globe*, © 2000; p. 119 Photo courtesy of Christine Root; p. 124 AP/Wide World Photos; p. 133 (top) FogStock LLC/Index Stock Imagery, (bottom) David Stoecklein/Corbis; p. 146 Photo courtesy of Brian Cantrill; p. 150 Photo courtesy of Jonathan LaRosa; p. 151 Photo courtesy of William Millerson; p. 155 Photo courtesy of Christine Root; p. 157 Photo courtesy of Christine Root; p. 164 B. & C. Alexander/Photo Researchers, Inc.; p. 168 (a) Photo courtesy of Christine Root; (b) Frank Siteman/Index Stock Imagery, (c) Photo courtesy of Christine Root; (d) Eric Sanford/Index Stock Imagery; p. 170 www.boulderteahouse.com.
Text credits: See page x

Library of Congress Cataloging-in-Publication Data
Blanchard, Karen Lourie
    For your information 1 / Karen Blanchard and Christine Root.—2nd ed.
      p. cm.
    ISBN 0-13-199186-8 (student book 1: alk. paper)—ISBN 0-13-199182-5 (student book 2: alk. paper)—ISBN 0-13-238008-0 (student book 3: alk. paper)—ISBN 0-13-243694-9 (student book 4: alk. paper)
    1. English language—Textbooks for foreign speakers. 2. Readers.
I. Root, Christine Baker. II. Title.
PE1128.B586 2006
428.6'4—dc22
                                               2006011193

Printed in the United States
7 8 9 10—V001—15 14 13 12

We dedicate this book to our boys,
the lights of our lives.

CONTENTS

Scope and Sequence

UNIT	CHAPTER	READING SELECTION	READING SKILL
1 **ALL IN THE FAMILY**	Chapter 1	A Family Bike Trip	Scanning for Information
	Chapter 2	What's in a Name?	Thinking about What You Know
	Chapter 3	The Jim Twins	Making a Chart

ⓐⓑⓒNEWS Video Excerpt: Amazing Family

UNIT	CHAPTER	READING SELECTION	READING SKILL
2 **LET'S EAT**	Chapter 1	A Peanut Butter Restaurant	Reading with a Purpose
	Chapter 2	The Tokyo Fish Market	
	Chapter 3	A Cookie with a Surprise Inside	Predicting Making a Chart

ⓐⓑⓒNEWS Video Excerpt: Fish Artist

UNIT	CHAPTER	READING SELECTION	READING SKILL
3 **KEEPING IN TOUCH**	Chapter 1	Sending E-Cards	Predicting
	Chapter 2	Easy Ways To Keep in Touch	
	Chapter 3	Sending Cyber-Hugs	

ⓐⓑⓒNEWS Video Excerpt: Congo the Painting Chimp

UNIT	CHAPTER	READING SELECTION	READING SKILL
4 **THE WORK WORLD**	Chapter 1	What's New?	Reading with a Purpose
	Chapter 2	A Job Change	Skimming for the Main Idea
	Chapter 3	A Popular Cartoonist	Reading with a Purpose

ⓐⓑⓒNEWS Video Excerpt: Human Cannonball

VOCABULARY SKILL	APPLICATION SKILL
Organizing Words	Improving Your Reading Speed
Learning Cardinal and Ordinal Numbers	Writing a Journal Entry
Learning Compound Words	Reading a Birth Announcement
Learning Synonyms Organizing Words	Reading a Menu Improving Your Reading Speed
Understanding Word Parts: The Suffix –y	Writing a Journal Entry
Learning Antonyms	
Learning Synonyms and Antonyms	Reading a Calendar
Learning Expressions with *Make*	Improving Your Reading Speed
Learning Phrasal Verbs with *Put*	Writing a Journal Entry
Learning Synonyms Organizing Words	Taking a Survey
Understanding Word Parts: The Suffix –er Learning Expressions with *Take*	Reading Ads Writing a Journal Entry
Understanding Word Parts: The Suffix –ist	

Scope and Sequence

VOCABULARY SKILL	APPLICATION SKILL
Understanding Word Parts: The Prefix *dis–*	Reading Charts Understanding Symbols Writing a Journal Entry
Understanding Word Parts: The Suffix *–ish*	
Understanding Word Parts: The Prefix *un–*	
Learning Phrasal Verbs	Reading a Map Understanding Headlines Taking a Survey Writing a Journal Entry
Learning Synonyms and Antonyms	
Understanding Pronouns	
Learning Expressions with *Take*	Reading Charts Improving Your Reading Speed Understanding Headlines Writing a Journal Entry Reading a TV Guide
Understanding Word Parts: The Prefix *multi–*	
Understanding Word Forms	
Understanding Word Forms	Writing an E-mail Reading E-mails Writing a Journal Entry
Understanding Word Parts: The Prefix *re–*	
Understanding Word Parts: The Suffix *–ful*	

Text Credits

The FYI Approach

Welcome to *For Your Information,* a reading and vocabulary skill-building series for English language learners. The FYI series is based on the premise that students are able to read at a higher level of English than they can produce. An important goal of the texts is to help students move beyond passive reading to become active, thoughtful, and confident readers of English.

This popular series is now in its second edition. The book numbers have changed in the new edition and include the following levels:

For Your Information 1	Beginning
For Your Information 2	High-Beginning
For Your Information 3	Intermediate
For Your Information 4	High-Intermediate

Each text in the FYI series is made up of eight thematically-based units containing three chapters, which are built around high-interest reading selections with universal appeal. The levels are tailored to help students increase their vocabulary base and build their reading skills. In addition to comprehension and vocabulary practice activities, reading and vocabulary building skills are presented throughout each chapter. Although FYI is a reading series, students also practice speaking, listening, and writing throughout the texts. In trademark FYI style, the tasks in all books are varied, accessible, and inviting, and they provide opportunities for critical thinking and for frequent interaction.

The Second Edition

The second edition of *For Your Information 1* features:

- new and updated reading selections
- designated target vocabulary words for study and practice
- expanded reading-skill-building activities
- vocabulary-building skills and word-attack activities
- a glossary of the target vocabulary words used in the readings
- a companion DVD of ABC News excerpts on related themes, with accompanying activities

Using FYI 1

UNITS

FYI 1 contains eight units, each with three chapters. Every unit begins with Points to Ponder questions and concludes with a Tie It All Together section and a Vocabulary Self-Test.

Points to Ponder

These prereading questions serve to introduce the theme of each unit and activate students' background knowledge before they begin the individual chapters.

CHAPTERS

The basic format for each chapter is as follows:

Before You Read

Each chapter opens with Before You Read, a selection of exercises designed to prime students for successful completion of the chapter. Target vocabulary words are introduced, as are background questions, activities, and prereading skills such as Predicting and Reading with a Purpose.

Reading

Each reading relates to the theme of the unit. For variety, the readings include articles, essays, and interviews, among other genres. Close attention has been paid to the level and length of the readings, which range from 250 to 450 words.

After You Read

Readings are followed by a combination of Comprehension Check questions and activities, along with Vocabulary Practice exercises that give students the opportunity to work with the target words from the reading. Introduction and reinforcement of reading and vocabulary skills also fall throughout this section. Talk It Over questions appear regularly, as do culminating activities that require students to practice real-life skills such as taking surveys, reading newspaper headlines, and writing messages and e-mails.

UNIT CONCLUSIONS

Tie It All Together

Each unit concludes with activities that encourage students to think about, distill, and consolidate the information they have absorbed throughout the unit. Among these Tie It All Together activities are discussion questions based on the general theme of the unit, an activity that is "Just for Fun," plus new activities based on a video excerpt related to the unit theme. This section also features the Reader's Journal, an opportunity for students to reflect, in writing, on the ideas in each unit. Space for each response is provided at the end of the book.

Vocabulary Self-Test

Each unit closes with a vocabulary self-test to help students review new words they've learned. Test answers are included at the back of the book, to allow students to check and assess their own answers.

References

The FYI approach is based on the following research and scholarship:

Campbell, Pat. *Teaching Reading to Adults: A Balanced Approach.* Edmonton: Grass Roots Press, 2003.

Drucker, Mary J. "What Reading Teachers Should Know about ESL Learners: Good Teaching Is Teaching for All. These Strategies Will Help English-Language Learners, but They Will Help Typical Learners as Well." *The Reading Teacher,* Vol. 57 (1), September 2003.

Pang, Elizabeth S., and Michael L. Kamil. *Second-Language Issues in Early Literacy and Instruction.* Stanford University: Publication Series No. 1, 2004.

Singhal, Meena. *Teaching Reading to Adult Second Language Learners: Theoretical Foundations, Pedagogical Applications, and Current Issues.* Lowell, MA: The Reading Matrix, 2005.

Acknowledgments

We have many people to thank for their contributions to this book. For their generosity of time and talent, we thank Lorraine and Alan Bressler, Linda Butler, Bryan Cantrill, Randy Glasbergen, Matt Kromer, Jonathan LaRosa, Moses Rifkin, Jeremy Schwartz, Doree Shafrir, Natalie Smith, and Roberta Steinberg.

At Pearson Education, we thank Laura Le Dréan and Mykan White for their attention to detail in editing the manuscript. We also thank Aerin Csigay for his care in photo research and Mindy DePalma for her skill in wending the manuscript through the production process.

Finally, deep appreciation to our families and friends for willingly reading the many articles we considered for this book and evaluating them for high interest.

KLB, CBR

About the Authors

Karen Blanchard and Christine Root first met when they were teaching at the University of Pennsylvania. It wasn't long before they began working on their first book, *Ready to Write*. They have continued their successful collaboration, producing more than seventeen popular reading and writing textbooks.

Karen has an M.S.Ed. in English Education from the University of Pennsylvania, and Christine has an M.Ed. in English Education from the University of Massachusetts, Boston. Both authors have over twenty-five years' experience working with English language learners at the university level. Karen has also taught at the American Language Academy at Beaver College, in addition to tutoring students at many levels. Christine has taught in the Harvard ESL program and is a founder, coordinator, and guide in the ESOL tour program at the Museum of Fine Arts, Boston. Karen and Christine continue to enjoy working together to create English language textbooks for students around the world.

ALL IN THE FAMILY

Families are an important part of every culture. In many countries, family is the most important thing in a person's life. In this unit, you will learn about some interesting families and family traditions.

Points to Ponder

Discuss these questions in a small group.

1. Look at the picture. What are the people doing? Do you think they are having a good time?

2. What activities do you like to do with your family?

3. Do you have any brothers or sisters? How old are they? What are their names?

A Family Bike Trip

Before You Read

A Discuss these questions with a partner.

1. Do you have a bicycle? How often do you ride it?
2. Do you like to take trips with your family? Why or why not?
3. What are some places you have traveled to with your family?

B Study these words from the article. Write each word next to the correct definition.

celebrated   daughters   disease

exciting   goal   special

1. *disease*	a sickness
2.	had a special meal or party for an important event
3.	better or more important than most things
4.	something you want to do or make happen
5.	making you feel very happy or interested
6.	female children

A FAMILY BIKE TRIP

1   The Eber family just took a trip around the world. The trip took sixteen months. Paula and Lorenz Eber and their **daughters**, Anya, fourteen years old, and Yvonne, twelve, rode their bikes more than 9,300 miles (about 15,000 kilometers). They rode their bikes in twenty-four countries. They rode in four continents: Europe, Asia, North America, and Australia.

A map of the Ebers' bike trip around the world

2   Why did the Ebers want to ride their bikes around the world? They had an important **goal**. They wanted to raise money to help people who have asthma. Asthma is a **disease** that makes it hard for people to breathe. Paula has had asthma since she was a child. Now, she helps other people who have asthma.

3   The Eber family started an organization[1] called World Bike for Breath. "Asthma is a big problem," Anya said. "The disease makes it difficult for over 150 million people all over the world to breathe." The Ebers want to teach people around the world about asthma. They also want to collect $5 million through World Bike for Breath. How will they raise the money? People and companies give money to their organization for each mile the family rides. The Ebers will use the money to find a cure[2] for asthma and to help children with asthma.

4   The Ebers take many bike trips, but this one was very **special**. One of the most **exciting** parts of the trip was having a Christmas dinner of Chinese duck in Hong Kong. They also **celebrated** Yvonne's twelfth birthday in Tonga, an island in the Pacific Ocean. They ate a coconut-and-mango birthday cake. The trip was exciting but difficult. The family had to sleep in tents[3] for most of the trip. The hardest part, Yvonne said, was the bad weather and the bugs.

The Ebers in front of the Great Wall of China

[1] **organization** – a group of people working for the same purpose

[2] **cure** – something that makes a sick person healthy again

[3] **tent** –

Comprehension Check

A Circle the correct answer.

1. Why did the Eber family ride their bikes around the world?
   a. to celebrate Yvonne's birthday
   b. to visit Hong Kong
   c. to raise money for asthma

2. What will the Ebers use the money for?
   a. to help people with asthma
   b. to take another trip around the world
   c. to buy a Christmas dinner

3. Where did the family usually sleep at night?
   a. in houses
   b. in tents
   c. on bikes

4. What was the hardest part of the trip for Yvonne?
   a. the bad weather and the bugs
   b. eating coconut-and-mango birthday cake
   c. helping people throughout the world to breathe

SKILL FOR SUCCESS

Scanning for Information
Scanning is a way to read quickly to find specific information such as a name or date. To scan, move your eyes quickly down the page until you find the information you need. Think about how the information will be presented. For example, if you are looking for a date, scan for numbers. Learning to scan will help you become a better reader.

B Scan the article for the answer to each question. Work as fast as you can.

1. How long did the trip take? _sixteen months_

2. How many countries did the Ebers visit? _____

3. How much money do the Ebers want to raise? _____

4. How many miles did they ride their bikes? _____

5. Where did Yvonne celebrate her twelfth birthday? _____

Vocabulary Practice

A Complete each sentence with the correct word.

celebrated	daughters	disease
exciting	goal	special

1. Yvonne _____ her birthday on the trip.

2. An _____ part of the trip was eating Christmas dinner in Hong Kong.

3. The Ebers take many bike trips, but this one was _____.

4. The Ebers and their two _____ took a trip around the world.

5. The _____ of their trip was to raise money for asthma.

6. Asthma is an example of a _____.

B Circle the correct answer.

1. When people <u>celebrate</u> something, they usually _____.
   a. have a good time
   b. have a bad time

2. When you do something <u>exciting</u>, you feel _____.
   a. sad
   b. happy

3. If your <u>goal</u> is to learn English, you _____.
   a. want to learn English
   b. don't care about learning English

4. Which is a <u>special</u> day?
   a. a baby's first birthday
   b. every Tuesday

5. Which is an example of a <u>disease</u>?
   a. asthma
   b. bad weather

6. If you have one <u>daughter</u> and two sons, you have _____.
   a. two boys and one girl
   b. one boy and two girls

Organizing Words

When you learn new words, it is helpful to put them into groups that have something in common. This helps you remember their meanings more easily.

C Read the list of family words. Organize the words by writing each one in the correct column. Use your dictionary to help you.

aunt	brother	child	cousin
daughter	father	husband	mother
nephew	niece	parent	sibling
sister	son	uncle	wife

Male	Female	Male or Female
	aunt	

Talk It Over

Discuss these questions as a class.

1. Do you or does anyone you know have asthma?
2. Have you ever helped raise money to help people with problems?
3. Would you like to travel around the world with your family? Why or why not?

What's in a Name?

Before You Read

A Discuss these questions with a partner.

1. Does your name have a special meaning? What does it mean?
2. Do you have the same name as anyone else in your family?
3. What are some common boys' names and girls' names in your country?
4. A nickname is a name your friends or family call you. Do you have a nickname? What is it?

B Study these words from the article. Write each word next to the correct definition.

choose   customs   honest
intelligent   popular

1.	to decide which thing you want
2.	truthful; not likely to lie or steal
3.	smart; able to learn and understand things easily
4.	ways of behaving that have been done for a long time
5.	liked by many people

Thinking about What You Know

Before you read, it is helpful to **think about what you already know** about the topic. You will better understand what you read when you connect the things you already know with the new information in the passage.

C You are going to read an article about how parents choose names for their children. Check the statements you think are true about names.

❏ 1. Customs for naming children are different around the world.

❏ 2. Some parents name a child after their own father or mother.

❏ 3. Naming a baby is not usually an important event.

❏ 4. Some people believe a baby's name has special power over his or her future.

❏ 5. Nicknames are popular in many cultures.

❏ 6. In some cultures, parents give a child two names.

❏ 7. Many people have parties to celebrate naming their child.

What's in a Name?

1 How do parents in your country **choose** names for their children? The **customs** for naming children are different in many countries. Here are just a few of the customs around the world.

2 Some people believe a baby's name has special power over his or her future. In some Middle-Eastern countries, parents choose a name that they hope will affect their child's future. For example, if parents want their daughter to have good luck, they might choose the name Saidah, which means *lucky* in Arabic. If they want the child to be very smart, they might name her Nabeeha, which means *intelligent*. In China, a boy's name may have meanings such as *strong* and **honest**. A girl's name might mean *pretty* or *kind*.

3 In some cultures, parents use the name of a family member when they name a baby. For example, Irish parents often name the first son after the father's father, and the second son after the mother's father. The first girl is named after the mother's mother, and the second girl after the father's mother. In other cultures, people don't name children after family members. Korean people, for example, never name a baby after a family member.

4 In some parts of Africa, such as Ghana, parents give a child two names. One name tells the day of the week the child was born. The other tells the child's place in the family. For example, the name Kofi Mensah means that the child was born on a Friday (Kofi) and is the third child (Mensah) in the family.

5   In most places around the world, naming babies is an important event. In China, people have a special party when they name their baby. The party happens one month after the baby is born. At the party, the parents announce the baby's name. Everyone enjoys a big meal and celebrates the baby's new name. In some parts of India, a naming celebration happens on the twelfth day after a baby's birth. Female friends and relatives come to a party, and the baby's name is chosen.

Chinese parents have a party to name their baby.
....

6   Nicknames are **popular** all over the world. A nickname is a name that your friends or family call you. Sometimes a nickname makes a long name shorter. For example, the nickname for Patricia is Pat. The nickname for Christopher is Chris. A nickname can also describe a person. Someone with curly hair might have the nickname Curly. A short person might have the nickname Shorty. Do you have a nickname? ■

After You Read

Comprehension Check

Read these statements. If a statement is true, write *T* on the line. If it is false, write *F.*

___*T*___ 1. Different countries have different customs for naming babies.

_____ 2. The Arabic name Saidah means *lucky.*

_____ 3. In all cultures, people name a baby after someone in their family.

_____ 4. Irish parents often name the first son after the mother's father.

_____ 5. In some countries, people have a party to celebrate the naming of a baby.

_____ 6. Nicknames are used only in the United States.

Vocabulary Practice

A Complete each sentence with the correct word.

choose   customs   honest
intelligent   popular

1. If parents want their child to be very smart, they might give her a name that means _____.

2. The _____ for naming children are different in many countries.

3. If parents want their daughter to have good luck, they might _____ the name Saidah. It means *lucky* in Arabic.

4. In China, a boy's name may have meanings such as _____, which means *truthful*.

5. Lots of people have nicknames. They are _____ in countries all over the world.

B Circle the correct answer.

1. If something is a <u>custom</u> in your country, people _____.
   a. just started doing it
   b. have done it for many years

2. If a name is <u>popular</u>, _____.
   a. only a few people have it
   b. many people have it

3. If someone is an <u>intelligent</u> person, he or she _____.
   a. can learn things easily
   b. has a hard time learning things

4. <u>Honest</u> people do not _____.
   a. tell the truth
   b. tell lies

5. When you are at a restaurant, what do you <u>choose</u>?
   a. something to eat
   b. something to write with

SKILL
FOR
SUCCESS

Learning Cardinal and Ordinal Numbers

Cardinal numbers express the number or amount of something.
2 (two) children; 25 (twenty-five) pounds

Ordinal numbers tell the order of something.
*We named our **first** daughter Megan and our **second** daughter Lisa.*

C Study the chart of cardinal and ordinal numbers. Then answer the questions that follow.

Cardinal Number	Word	Ordinal Number	Word
1	one	1st	first
2	two	2nd	second
3	three	3rd	third
4	four	4th	fourth
5	five	5th	fifth
9	nine	9th	ninth
17	seventeen	17th	seventeenth
22	twenty-two	22nd	twenty-second
61	sixty-one	61st	sixty-first

1. What is the *last* word in the *first* paragraph of What's in a Name?
   _____

2. What country is discussed in the *fourth* paragraph? _____

3. Which paragraph gives examples of Arabic names? (Use an ordinal number in your answer.) _____

Talk It Over

Discuss these questions as a class.

1. How do parents choose a name for their baby in your culture?
2. In your culture, do children have the same names as other family members?
3. In your country, is it common to have a party when a baby is named? Describe the party.

Chapter 2 **11**

Scan the birth announcement to answer these questions.

1. What is the baby's name? _____

2. How much did he weigh? _____

3. What time was the baby born? _____

4. What is the baby's birthday? _____

5. Who are his parents? _____

Great News! It's a Boy!

John and Sarah Miller

are Celebrating

the Birth of their New Son:

Michael Miller

Born: August 15, at 10:30A.M.

Weight: 8 pounds and 3 ounces

Length: 21 inches

The Jim Twins

Twins are two children born to the same mother at the same time. In this chapter, you will learn some amazing things about twins who met when they were thirty-nine years old.

Before You Read

A **Discuss these questions with a partner.**

1. Are you a twin, or do you know any twins? How are you (or they) the same or different?
2. Are there any twins in your family?
3. Do you think it would be fun to be a twin? Why or why not?

B **Study these words from the article. Write each word next to the correct definition.**

favorite   headache   hobby

similar   twice   vacation

1.	almost the same
2.	time away from work or school when you can travel or rest
3.	best liked
4.	an activity that you enjoy doing
5.	two times
6.	a pain you feel inside your head

The Jim Twins

1   When Jim Springer was thirty-nine years old, he learned he had a twin brother. His twin brother's name was Jim Lewis. The brothers were separated when they were four weeks old. They were adopted¹ by different families. They grew up in different towns. They didn't know or see each other for thirty-nine years!

2   Jim Springer decided to find his twin brother. He went to Jim Lewis's town and found his house. When he saw Jim Lewis, Jim Springer thought he was looking in a mirror! Both men were 6 feet (1.8 meters) tall and weighed 180 pounds (82 kilograms). They also had the same face and the same voice.

3   The twins grew up in different families, but they were **similar** in many ways. Jim Springer was married **twice**. Jim Lewis was married twice. Their first wives were both named Linda. Their second wives were both named Betty. Jim Lewis named his son James Alan. Jim Springer named his son James Allen. As children, both Jims had a pet dog, and both dogs were named Toy. In school, their **favorite** subject was math, and their least favorite was spelling. Both bit their fingernails. Both had a **headache** at the same time every day. Both Jims drove the same color and kind of car: a blue Chevrolet. In sports, they were alike, too. Both disliked baseball and liked football. The twins had the same job. They both worked as policemen. They even had the same **hobby**, making things with wood. Finally, both Jims took a **vacation** every year at the same beach in Florida.

4   The twins were very happy to finally meet each other. Jim Springer said something was missing from his life before he met his twin. Jim Lewis said the same thing. Now, they know what was missing. Now, they know *who* it was.

---

¹ **adopted** – taken into a new family to be part of that family

After You Read

Comprehension Check

A Read these statements. If a statement is true, write *T* on the line. If it is false, write *F*.

_____ 1. Jim Lewis and Jim Springer grew up in the same house.

_____ 2. Jim Springer is younger than Jim Lewis.

_____ 3. The twins are the same in many ways.

_____ 4. The Jim twins were very happy when they finally met.

SKILL FOR SUCCESS ✓

Making a Chart
Making a chart is a good way to make sure you understand and remember what you read.

B Complete the chart with information that is true about both Jims.

Height	6 feet
Weight	
First Wife's Name	
Second Wife's Name	
Pet's Name	
Favorite Subject	
Least Favorite Subject	
Job	
Hobby	
Vacation Spot	

F Y I

Identical twins look just the same. One set of identical twins is born in every 285 births.

Vocabulary Practice

A Complete each sentence with the correct word.

favorite   headache   hobby   similar   twice   vacation

1. The twins had the same _____, making things with wood.

2. Both Jims went to Florida for their _____.

3. Jim Springer's _____ class in school was math.

4. Jim Springer and Jim Lewis grew up in different families, but they were _____ in many ways.

5. Both Jims had a _____ at the same time every day.

6. Jim Lewis was married _____, and so was his twin brother.

B Circle the correct answer.

1. Which is an example of a <u>vacation</u>?

   a. a trip to the mountains

   b. a week at your job

2. If you went to the same place <u>twice</u>, you went there _____.

   a. three times

   b. two times

3. Which is an example of a <u>hobby</u>?

   a. taking pictures for money

   b. taking pictures for fun

4. If something is your <u>favorite</u> food, you _____.

   a. like it a lot

   b. don't like it

5. If two people are <u>similar</u>, they are _____.

   a. very different

   b. the same in many ways

C Ask and answer these questions with a partner.

1. What is (or was) your <u>favorite</u> class in school?
2. What do you do when you have a <u>headache</u>?
3. Do you have a <u>hobby</u>? What is it?
4. Are you more <u>similar</u> to your mother or your father?
5. What is your <u>favorite</u> place to go on <u>vacation</u>?

Learning Compound Words

A **compound word** is made of two or more words. For example, *headache* is a compound word. It is made of the words *head* (the part of your body) and *ache* (a pain). If you know the meanings of these two words, you can guess what *headache* means.

In this chapter, you learned several compound words: *headache, fingernails, baseball, football, policemen.*

D Complete each sentence with the correct compound word(s). Use your dictionary to help you.

baseball   fingernails   football   headache   policemen

1. The _____ were very helpful. We called them when we had a car accident.

2. I usually cut my _____ once a week.

3. The music was very loud. It gave me a _____.

4. My favorite sports are _____ and _____.

Improve Your Reading Speed

Look at the first word in each row. Circle the words that are the same as the first word. Work as fast as you can.

1. **son**	ton	(son)	sun	sons	non	(son)	(son)
2. **year**	year	hear	dear	year	fear	yell	yard
3. **wife**	life	wolf	wife	wire	wife	safe	wife
4. **fun**	run	fame	fan	run	fun	fund	funny
5. **house**	hour	houses	house	hunger	mouse	hunt	hot
6. **party**	pantry	part	partly	party	pink	paste	porter
7. **grew**	grew	grew	grow	grew	gray	grew	grew
8. **sports**	sport	sports	spots	sports	sports	spores	sports
9. **four**	four	for	four	foul	four	four	four
10. **week**	week	week	weak	week	weeks	week	seek

Find Someone Who . . .

Ask your classmates about their families. Find one person who matches each description. Write that person's name in the chart.

Find someone who . . .	Classmate's Name
has an older brother.	
is an only child (has no brothers or sisters).	
is the oldest child.	
is the youngest child.	
has a younger sister.	
has more than five brothers and sisters.	
has a niece or nephew.	
has more than ten cousins.	
has twins in his or her family.	
has an older sister.	

Tie It All Together

Discussion

Discuss these questions in a small group.

1. Do you think friends are more important than family? Why or why not?
2. How did your parents choose your name?

Just for Fun

Put the letters in order to form a word. All of the words are about families.

1. wtsni   _twins_

2. othbrre   _____

3. celnu   _____

4. greadtuh   _____

5. starpen   _____

6. siucno   _____

Video Activity

Amazing Family

You will see a video about a family with twenty-five adopted sons. What do you think life is like in this family?

A Study these words and phrases. Then watch the video.

   adopted   disabled   obstacles

B Read these statements and then watch the video again. If a statement is true, write *T* on the line. If it is false, write *F*.

_____ 1. All of the Silcocks' children are adopted.

_____ 2. Each member of the family eats thirty eggs for breakfast.

_____ 3. The Silcock family has a business that sells gas.

_____ 4. The government gives the Silcocks money to help raise their sons.

C Discuss these questions with a partner or in a small group.

What are the advantages of living in a large family? A small family?

Reader's Journal

At the end of every unit, you will write in the Reader's Journals on pages 187–190. Don't worry about spelling, grammar, or punctuation.

Think about the topics and ideas you have read about and discussed in this unit. Choose a topic and write about it for ten to twenty minutes. Pick a topic from the following list, or choose one of your own.

- why families are important
- taking a vacation with your family
- what your name means

Vocabulary Self-Test

Complete each sentence with the correct word.

A choose   goal   honest
       popular   twice   vacation

1. He always tells the truth. He is very _____.

2. The company did well this year. It reached its sales _____.

3. John is a _____ boys' name in the United States.

4. Hamza is going to be on _____ in Spain for two weeks.

5. Please help me _____ which dress to wear to the party. I can't decide.

6. I've seen that movie _____, and I enjoyed it both times.

B celebrate   disease   exciting
       favorite   intelligent

1. Delma gets excellent grades in school. She is very _____ and studies hard.

2. We always _____ my father's birthday at the same restaurant.

3. I painted my room blue. It's my _____ color.

4. My aunt is very sick. She has heart _____.

5. The soccer game was very _____. Our team won in the last minute.

C customs   headache   hobby
       similar   special

1. Different countries have different wedding _____.

2. I gave my mother a _____ gift for her fiftieth birthday.

3. Chin's _____ is playing guitar.

4. My two sisters look _____. They both have brown hair and green eyes.

5. If I don't wear my glasses, I get a _____.

LET'S EAT

Food is necessary for life. Food is also one of life's pleasures. In this unit, you will read about a fun restaurant, a big fish market, and the history of a cookie.

Points to Ponder

Discuss these questions in a small group.

1. Look at the picture. What is the woman doing?

2. What are some of your favorite foods?

3. What do you usually eat for breakfast? Lunch? Dinner?

4. Do you like to try new foods? Why or why not?

A Peanut Butter Restaurant

Before You Read

A Discuss these questions with a partner.

1. Have you ever eaten peanut butter? Did you like it?
2. Is peanut butter a popular food in your country?
3. Sandwiches are a popular lunch food in the United States. Are sandwiches popular in your country? Do you like them?
4. Peanut-butter-and-jelly sandwiches are one of the most popular sandwiches in the United States. Have you ever had a peanut-butter-and-jelly sandwich? Did you like it?

B Think about the three questions in the chart. Check the box with the correct answer. Then compare answers with a partner.

	Once a month	Once a week	Two or three times a week	Other
How often do you eat breakfast in a restaurant?				
How often do you eat lunch in a restaurant?				
How often do you eat dinner in a restaurant?				

C Study these words from the article. Write each word next to the correct definition.

cookbook   dessert   menu

recipes   unusual

1.	not common
2.	a list of the food served in a restaurant
3.	a sweet food that you eat after a meal
4.	a book that tells you how to make and cook foods
5.	instructions that tell you how to cook things

SKILL FOR SUCCESS

Reading with a Purpose

Good readers have a **purpose,** or reason, for reading. Before you read, it is helpful good to think about questions you want the reading to answer. Then look for answers to those questions as you read.

D You are going to read about an interesting restaurant. What are three things you hope to learn from the article?

1. _____

2. _____

3. _____

A Peanut Butter Restaurant

1 Lee Zalben loves peanut butter. In fact, he loves it so much that he opened a restaurant in New York City called Peanut Butter & Co. You can probably guess what the restaurant serves. It serves all kinds of food made with peanut butter. Peanut Butter & Co. is open for lunch and dinner.

2 **Peanut Butter & Co**. has an interesting **menu**. Sandwiches are the most popular items. Of course, you can find peanut butter–and–jelly sandwiches on the menu. But you can also find lots of other **unusual** peanut butter sandwiches. For example, there is a peanut butter, cream cheese, and chocolate sandwich. There is also a peanut butter sandwich with bacon, lettuce, and tomato. One of the most popular sandwiches is called The Elvis. It is named after Elvis Presley. The Elvis

Lee Zalben loves peanut butter, so he opened a peanut butter restaurant.

....

A restaurant for peanut butter lovers

....

is a grilled peanut butter sandwich with honey and bananas. It was Elvis's favorite sandwich.

3   Most sandwiches cost about $5 or $6. Does that sound like a lot to pay for a peanut butter sandwich? The people who eat at Peanut Butter & Co. say $5 is a good price for lunch in New York.

4   Peanut Butter & Co. also serves **dessert** and drinks. Most of the desserts have peanut butter in them. Lots of people love the peanut butter cookies. The chocolate peanut butter pie is another well-liked dessert. Milkshakes[1] are popular drinks on the menu. All of the milkshakes have peanut butter in them.

5   Lee makes and sells his own peanut butter. You can buy it in food shops and grocery stores all over the country. You can also buy his peanut butter on his website, www.peanutbutterco.com. Lee recently wrote a **cookbook**. *The Peanut Butter & Co. Cookbook* has more than eighty **recipes**. Of course, every recipe uses peanut butter. ■

[1] **milkshakes** – drinks made of milk and ice cream

After You Read

Comprehension Check

A Write the correct paragraph number to answer each question.

1. Which paragraph discusses the price of sandwiches? _____

2. Which paragraph gives examples of desserts? _____

3. Which paragraph describes the menu? _____

4. Which paragraph talks about Zalben's cookbook? _____

B Read these statements. If a statement is true, write *T* on the line. If it is false, write *F*.

_____ 1. Lee Zalben loves peanut butter.

_____ 2. Peanut Butter & Co. serves breakfast, lunch, and dinner.

_____ 3. Peanut Butter & Co. is in New York City.

_____ 4. Peanut Butter & Co. serves sandwiches and desserts.

_____ 5. Peanut butter and chocolate is the most popular sandwich at Peanut Butter & Co.

_____ 6. Most of the sandwiches at Peanut Butter & Co. cost $10.

_____ 7. You can buy Lee Zalben's peanut butter only on his website.

_____ 8. Lee wrote a cookbook with recipes that include peanut butter.

Vocabulary Practice

A Complete each sentence with the correct word(s).

cookbook   dessert   menu
recipes   unusual

1. All of the _____ in Lee's _____ use peanut butter.

2. Lots of people order the peanut butter cookies for _____.

3. Peanut Butter & Co. has an interesting _____. You can order many different kinds of sandwiches.

4. Peanut Butter & Co. serves the usual peanut-butter-and-jelly sandwich. There are also many _____ kinds of peanut butter sandwiches, such as the peanut butter, cream cheese, and chocolate sandwich.

B Circle the correct answer.

1. Which is a <u>dessert</u>?
   a. a cheese sandwich
   b. a piece of cake

2. If you want to find a <u>recipe</u> for chocolate peanut butter pie, where would you look?
   a. on a menu
   b. in a cookbook

3. If a kind of food is <u>unusual</u>, it is _____.
   a. common
   b. not common

4. What would you probably find on a breakfast <u>menu</u>?
   a. eggs
   b. pizza

SKILL FOR SUCCESS

Learning Synonyms

Synonyms are words that have the same meaning. For example, *big* and *large* are synonyms. Learning synonyms can help you expand your vocabulary and become a better reader.

C Use the list below to write the correct synonym for each word from the article.

named   popular   purchase   types

Word	Synonym
called	1. *named*
kinds	2.
well-liked	3.
buy	4.

D Complete the paragraph using the synonyms from the chart in Exercise C.

The Glenside Bakery sells many _____ of desserts. One of

the most _____ desserts is _____ Dan's Dream

Bar. It is a peanut butter brownie covered with chocolate. Every time I go

to the Glenside Bakery, I _____ at least two Dream Bars.

✓ **Organizing Words**

E Read the list of food and drink words. Organize the words by putting them into groups. Write each word in the correct box. Use your dictionary to help you.

bacon	banana	beef	broccoli
carrots	chicken	chocolate	coffee
cookies	honey	juice	lettuce
milk	orange	peach	pie
soda	spinach	tea	turkey

Fruit	Vegetables	Meat	Desserts or Sweet Things	Drinks

Make a Cookbook   Follow these instructions to make a class cookbook.

1. Choose your favorite dish.
2. Make a list of ingredients.
3. Write instructions for making the dish. Make the directions as easy to follow as you can.
4. Make a copy of your recipe for every person in your class.
5. Combine all the recipes.
6. With your classmates, think of a title for your class cookbook and make a cover.

Read a Menu

Scan the menu below to answer these questions.

1. How much does a large traditional pizza cost? _____
2. How many kinds of toppings does Marco's have? _____
3. Which sandwich costs the most? _____
4. How much does a garden salad cost? _____
5. Which beverage costs the least? _____
6. How much does a small pizza with olives cost? _____
7. How much does a large pizza with sliced tomatoes and onions cost? _____

Marco's Pizza Shop

Pizza

Marco's Traditional Pizza with Tomato Sauce and Cheese

Small $8.00	Medium $10.00	Large $11.50

Toppings $2.00 each

Sliced Tomatoes	Olives	Eggplant	Onions
Red Peppers	Mushrooms	Anchovies	Spinach

Combination of 2 Toppings $2.50   Combination of 3 Toppings $5.00   Extra Cheese $1.50

Burgers and Sandwiches

Hamburger $5.50	Sliced Turkey Sandwich $7.00
Cheeseburger $5.90	Salami Sandwich $6.75
Meatball $6.75	Tuna Sandwich $7.50
Grilled Chicken $6.75	Grilled Vegetable Wrap $7.75

Salads

Garden Salad $5.75
Greek Salad $7.00

Beverages

Soda $1.50	Bottled Water $1.50
Coffee $1.00	Iced Tea $1.50

The Tokyo Fish Market

Before You Read

A Discuss these questions with a partner.

1. Do you like to eat fish? What is your favorite kind of fish?
2. Is fish a popular food in your country?
3. How often do you eat fish?

B Study these words from the article. Write each word next to the correct definition.

famous   huge   noisy

seafood   smelly

1.	known and liked by many people
2.	ocean animals that can be eaten
3.	making or having loud sounds
4.	very big
5.	having a bad smell

THE TOKYO FISH MARKET

1   Two days ago, a tuna fish was swimming in the Atlantic Ocean near Boston. An American fishing boat caught it. The fishermen quickly froze the tuna. Then an airplane flew it to a **famous** fish market in Tokyo, Japan. The name of the fish market is Tsukiji. The tuna fish was the 197th tuna to arrive at Tsukiji that day.

Tuna Number 197 weighed 622 pounds (282 kg).

2   Tsukiji is the largest fish market in the world. It sells more than 2,000 kinds of **seafood** to restaurants and supermarkets all over Japan. The seafood comes from sixty different countries. Tsukiji sells about 5 million pounds (2.27 million kilograms) of seafood every day. People spend $28 million on fish there daily!

3   Tsukiji is like a small town. More than 60,000 people work there. The people are friendly, and they work very hard. They all work together to move fish as fast as possible from the sea to the dinner plate. The market opens at 4:00 A.M. It is a very busy place. Thousands of trucks, motorcycles, carts, and bicycles move people and fish around the **huge** building. Tsukiji is very **noisy**, but it is not **smelly**. People buy the seafood quickly, so there is no time for Tsukiji to smell bad.

After You Read

Comprehension Check

A Read these statements. If a statement is true, write *T* on the line. If it is false, write *F*.

_____ 1. Tsukiji is a small fish market in Japan.

_____ 2. Tsukiji sells seafood to restaurants and supermarkets.

_____ 3. All of the seafood at Tsukiji comes from Japan.

_____ 4. Tsukiji is noisy and smelly.

_____ 5. Seafood stays at Tsukiji for a long time before people buy it.

B Scan the article to match each question with the correct answer.

	Question		Answer
_c_	**1.** How much money do people spend daily at Tsukiji?	**a.**	4:00 A.M.
____	**2.** How much did Tuna Number 197 weigh?	**b.**	2,000
____	**3.** How many pounds of seafood do people buy every day at Tsukiji?	**c.**	$28 million
____	**4.** What time does the market open?	**d.**	more than 60,000
____	**5.** How many people work at Tsukiji?	**e.**	622 pounds
____	**6.** How many types of seafood does the market sell?	**f.**	5 million

Vocabulary Practice

A Complete each sentence with the correct word.

famous   huge   noisy   seafood   smelly

1. The Tokyo fish market sells more than 2,000 different kinds of _____.

2. There are thousands of people, trucks, and motorcycles in the market, so it is very _____.

3. The fish market is _____ all over the world.

4. Tsukiji is not _____, because people buy the seafood there so quickly.

5. Tsukiji is _____. In fact, it's the biggest fish market in the world.

B Cross out the word in each group that does not belong.

1. famous ~~old~~ well-known

2. loud noisy quiet

3. seafood fish bread

4. small large huge

SKILL FOR SUCCESS

Understanding Word Parts: The Suffix -y

A **suffix** is a letter or group of letters added to the end of a word to form another word. **The suffix -y** is added to a noun to form an adjective and means, *full of,* or *covered in.* For example, the word *noisy* from the article means *full of noise.*

C Complete each sentence with the correct word(s) ending in the suffix *-y.* Use your dictionary to help you.

cloudy   curly   dirty   rainy
sleepy   sunny   thirsty

1. I walk to work even on _____ days. I just take an umbrella.

2. Jana and her mother both have brown eyes and _____ hair.

3. You look very _____. You should go to bed early tonight.

4. I need something to drink. I'm _____.

5. Please take off your shoes before you come in the house. They are

    _____.

6. It was bright and _____ in the morning. But now it's

    getting _____.

Discuss these questions as a class.

1. Are there many fish markets in your country? Describe one of them. Is it big? How many types of seafood does it sell?
2. Would you like to visit Tsukiji? Why or why not?

Improve Your Reading Speed

Look at the first word in each row. Circle the words that are the same as the first word. Work as fast as you can.

1. **days**	bays	dogs	day	days	days	delay	days
2. **name**	came	name	nape	same	none	noun	name
3. **sea**	see	bee	seat	sea	seat	lead	see
4. **fast**	fast	feast	last	fat	fist	feast	fast
5. **smell**	smile	smell	sell	small	smelt	smell	smelly
6. **cake**	cake	care	make	cake	sake	cake	cake
7. **fish**	fish	fist	fifth	fish	flash	fish	wish
8. **town**	down	town	tows	tons	town	gown	town
9. **boat**	boar	bone	bat	boat	bait	boat	bolt
10. **kinds**	kids	kinds	kinds	kings	finds	kilns	killed

A Cookie with a Surprise Inside

Before You Read

A fortune cookie is a cookie with a small piece of paper inside. A fortune is printed on the paper. The fortune tells about your future. In this chapter, you will learn about the history of fortune cookies.

A Discuss these questions with a partner.

1. Do you usually eat dessert? Is dessert common in your country?
2. Do you like cookies? What is your favorite cookie?
3. Have you ever eaten a fortune cookie?

B Study these words from the article. Write each word next to the correct definition.

fired   handmade   invented
neighborhood   note

1.	made something for the first time
2.	a small area of town where people live
3.	made by a person, not by a machine
4.	ordered to leave a job
5.	a short piece of writing

Predicting

Before you read a passage, look it over to help you **predict** (guess) what it will be about. Predicting will help you understand what you read more easily.

C Follow these steps to make predictions about the article on page 36.

1. Think about the title and subtitle. Write them on the lines.

_____

_____

2. Read the four headings. Write them on the lines.

_____

_____

_____

_____

3. Look at the picture and read the caption (the words near the picture).

4. Check the ideas you think will be discussed in the article.

   ❏ **a.** who invented fortune cookies

   ❏ **b.** where fortune cookies are made

   ❏ **c.** how to make tea

   ❏ **d.** when fortune cookies were invented

   ❏ **e.** kinds of Chinese food

A Cookie with a Surprise Inside

Title →

Subtitle → *The History of the Fortune Cookie*

1 Fortune cookies are a popular dessert in Chinese restaurants in the United States. But fortune cookies are not from China. In fact, the first fortune cookies arrived in China in 1992. They came from Brooklyn, New York. They were called "genuine[1] American fortune cookies." We know that fortune cookies were first made in California. But no one knows for sure who **invented** them. Here are some stories about the history of fortune cookies.

Fortune cookies are served in Chinese-American restaurants. ← Caption

....

A Chinese-American Inventor? ← Heading

2 Over ninety years ago, a Chinese man named David Jung owned a restaurant in Los Angeles. According to one story, Jung made the first fortune cookies in 1918. He made them for poor people who lived in his **neighborhood.** Each cookie had a small piece of paper inside. The paper had words written on it. Jung hoped the words would make the unhappy people feel better. A few years later, Jung opened the Hong Kong Noodle Company. He made fortune cookies there.

A Japanese-American Inventor? ← Heading

3 Another story is that a Japanese man named Makoto Hagiwara invented the first fortune cookie in 1914. Hagiwara worked in San Francisco at the famous Japanese Tea Garden in Golden Gate Park. One day he was **fired** from his job. Many people helped him get his job back. Hagiwara wanted to thank the people who had helped

---

[1] **genuine** – real and true

him. He made cookies. Each cookie had a thank-you **note** inside. He gave the cookies to people who visited the Japanese Tea Garden.

Making the Cookies ← Heading

4 For many years, fortune cookies were **handmade**. That changed in 1964. Edward Louie owned the Lotus Fortune Cookie Company. He invented a new machine that made the cookies and put the fortunes inside. It made fortune cookies very quickly, so more people could enjoy them.

Fortune Cookies Today ← Heading

5 Today, the world's largest fortune cookie maker is Wonton Food, Inc. It is located in Queens, New York. It sells 60 million cookies a month! In addition, more than 100 other companies make millions of fortune cookies every day. Now, some companies even make fortunes in two languages: English/Spanish and English/Chinese.

After You Read

Comprehension Check

A Read these statements. If a statement is true, write *T* on the line. If it is false, write *F*.

_____ 1. Fortune cookies were invented in New York.

_____ 2. No one is sure who invented the first fortune cookie.

_____ 3. All fortune cookies have thank-you notes inside.

_____ 4. Many Chinese restaurants in the United States serve fortune cookies.

_____ 5. Today, fortune cookies are made by hand.

_____ 6. All fortunes are written in English and Spanish.

B Circle the correct answer.

1. Who made cookies for poor people?
   a. Makoto Hagiwara
   b. Edward Louie
   c. David Jung

2. Who worked at the famous Japanese Tea Garden?

    a. Makoto Hagiwara

    b. Edward Louie

    c. David Jung

3. What did Edward Louie invent?

    a. a machine that made fortune cookies

    b. the first fortune cookie

    c. Golden Gate Park

4. Where is the world's largest fortune cookie maker?

    a. China

    b. New York

    c. Los Angeles

✓ **Making a Chart**

C The article discusses two stories about the invention of fortune cookies. Complete the chart with information from the article.

	Story One	Story Two
Inventor's Name	David Jung	
Inventor's Job		
Place of Invention		
Year of Invention		
Reason for Invention		

Vocabulary Practice

A Complete each sentence with the correct word.

fired   handmade   invented   neighborhood   note

1. Jung made cookies for people who lived in his _____.

2. No one knows for sure who _____ the first fortune cookie.

3. After Makoto Hagiwara was _____, many people helped him get his job back.

4. The first fortune cookies were _____. Now, they are made by machines.

5. Each cookie had a thank-you _____ inside.

B Write the correct word to replace each underlined phrase.

fired   handmade   invented   neighborhood   note

1. Lewis arrived late to his job every day, so he was not allowed to work there anymore. _____

2. I wrote a short letter to my sister. I wanted to thank her for the flowers she sent me. _____

3. There are several good Chinese restaurants in my area of town. _____

4. Edward Louie first made the machine that puts fortunes in cookies. _____

5. Our fortune cookies are made by our own hands. They are not made by machine. _____ , _____ ?

SKILL FOR SUCCESS

Learning Antonyms

Antonyms are words that have opposite meanings. For example, *hot* and *cold* are antonyms. Learning antonyms can help you expand your vocabulary and become a better reader.

C Use the list below to write the correct Antonym for each word from the Article.

happy   outside   rich   smallest   worse

Word	Antonym
inside	1.
poor	2.
unhappy	3.
better	4.
largest	5.

D Complete each sentence with the correct antonym from the chart in Exercise C.

1. I started to feel sick yesterday. Today, I feel _____. I can't go to work.

2. This kind of car is only for _____ people. It costs a lot of money.

3. The little boy is smiling. He must be _____.

4. This cell phone fits in my pocket. It's the _____ one I've ever had.

5. The _____ of the house is painted red.

Unscramble
Fortunes

Complete the fortunes below by writing the words in the correct order.

1. good   will   you   luck   have

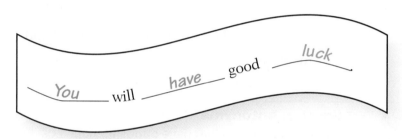

You ___ will ___ _have_ ___ good ___ _luck_ .

2. in   your   is   happiness   future

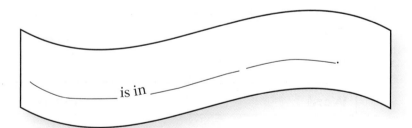

_____ is in _____ .

3. will   take   very   you   a   soon   trip

_____ will _____ a _____ very _____ .

4. enjoy   you   will   health   good

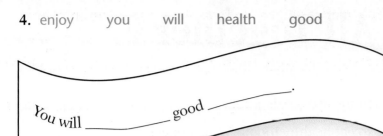

You will _____ good _____.

5. a   will   you   visit   place   new   soon

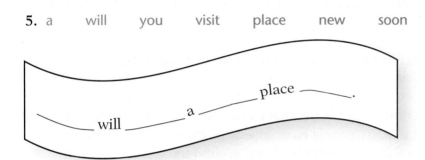

_____ will _____ a _____ place _____.

6. news   good   coming   to   is   you   year   this

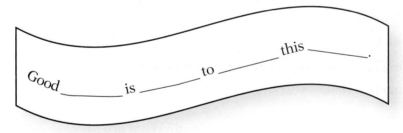

Good _____ is _____ to _____ this _____.

7. meet   you   a   will   friend   new

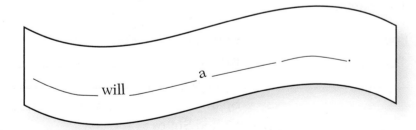

_____ will _____ a _____ _____.

Tie It All Together

F Y I

The average person in the United States visits a fast-food restaurant six times a month.

Discuss these questions in a small group.

1. Do you like to eat healthy foods? Which ones?

2. Food that is not very healthy but is quick and easy to eat is called junk food. Do you like junk food? What kind? How often do you eat it?

3. Do you like to shop for food in large supermarkets or in small shops? Why?

4. A superstition is a belief that some actions are lucky and others are unlucky. Many people have superstitions about foods. Read and discuss these superstitions from around the world. Use your dictionary to look up words you don't know.

   a. If you spill salt, you will have bad luck.

   b. If two women pour tea from the same pot, one of them will have a baby soon.

   c. Garlic keeps bad luck away.

   d. Eating an apple a day keeps the doctor away.

   e. Eating fish makes you smart.

5. Do you have any superstitions about food? What are they?

Just for Fun

Different countries are famous for different foods. Write a food that each country is famous for. Add more countries and foods to the list. Share your list with your classmates.

Country	Food	Country	Food
Brazil	_____	Korea	_____
China	_____	Mexico	_____
France	_____	Spain	_____
Italy	_____	United States	_____
Japan	_____		

Fish Artist

This video is about a man who makes art out of fish. What do you think his art will look like? What other types of unusual art do you know about?

A Study these words and phrases. Then watch the video.

celebrity   famous   immigrant

Famous Artists

Pablo Picasso   Vincent Van Gogh

B Read these statements and then watch the video again. Circle the correct answer.

1. Fernando Lara works at _____.
   a. an art museum   b. a seafood restaurant
   c. a food market

2. Lara's art _____.
   a. costs a lot of money to make   b. takes four years to make
   c. is made of old fish

3. People in the neighborhood _____.
   a. buy Lara's art   b. enjoy Lara's art
   c. eat Lara's art

C Discuss these questions with a partner or in a small group.

1. Do you think it would be more interesting to make art from fish or from paint? Why?
2. Do you think art is a good way for a store to attract customers? Why or why not?
3. Do you know of a store that attracts customers in an unusual way? How does it attract them?

Reader's Journal
Think about the topics and ideas you have read about and discussed in this unit. Choose a topic and write about it for ten to twenty minutes. Pick a topic from the following list, or choose one of your own.

• your favorite food   • trying new foods   • your favorite restaurant

Vocabulary Self-Test

Complete each sentence with the correct word.

A cookbook   fired   neighborhood
       seafood   smelly

1. I bought a _____ to learn how to make Japanese food.

2. Shin's favorite _____ is shrimp.

3. There are many good restaurants in Abdullah's _____.

4. That cheese is really _____, but it tastes very good.

5. The company _____ five workers last week.

B dessert   huge   invented
       noisy   recipe

1. Who _____ the lightbulb?

2. Marc doesn't like that restaurant. He says it's too _____.

3. My favorite _____ is blueberry pie with ice cream.

4. Sherry has a great _____ for vegetable soup.

5. Bruno and his wife just bought a _____ house. It has six bedrooms.

C famous   handmade   menu
       note   unusual

1. It is nice to send a thank-you _____ when someone gives you a gift.

2. I love this sweater. It was _____ in Peru.

3. Leonardo da Vinci's *Mona Lisa* is one of the most _____ paintings in the world.

4. This looks like a nice restaurant. Let's see what's on the _____ for tonight.

5. That baseball team has an _____ number of excellent players.

KEEPING IN TOUCH

English speakers use the expression *keep in touch* to mean *communicate with someone often*. In this unit, you will read about some of the many ways to keep in touch with friends and family.

"Got your e-mail, thanks."

Points to Ponder

Discuss these questions in a small group.

1. Look at the cartoon above. What do you think the people are doing? Do you think the cartoon is funny? Why or why not?

2. Do you think it is important to keep in touch with people? Why or why not?

3. How do you keep in touch with your friends and family? By phone? Letters? E-mail?

4. How often do you use e-mail?

Sending E-Cards

Before You Read

A Discuss these questions with a partner.

1. Are greeting cards popular in your country?
2. Do you like funny cards? Serious cards? Handmade cards?
3. Do you ever make cards to send to your family and friends?

B Answer the questions in the chart by checking *Yes* or *No.* Then compare answers with a partner.

	Yes	No
1. Do you send greeting cards to your friends and family?		
2. Do you send postcards when you travel?		
3. Have you ever sent a card or postcard from your computer?		
4. Have you ever received a card or postcard on your computer?		
5. Have you ever received an invitation to a party on your computer?		

C Study these words from the article. Write each word next to the correct definition.

educational   free   graduation

inexpensive   message

1.	low in price
2.	not costing any money
3.	a small amount of information that you send to someone
4.	helping you to learn
5.	the time when you complete school and receive a diploma or degree

✓ **Predicting**

D Follow these steps to make predictions about the article on page 48.

1. Think about the title. Write it on the line.

   _____

2. Read the two headings. Write them on the lines.

   _____

   _____

3. Look at the picture and read the caption.

4. What do you think the article will be about? Discuss your ideas with a partner.

Sending E-Cards

1 Lots of people like to send greeting cards. Many people send cards to family and friends on holidays and birthdays. They also send thank-you cards, get-well cards, anniversary cards, and **graduation** cards. In fact, there are cards for almost every event. And when they travel, many people send postcards to their family and friends.

Many people use a computer to send e-cards.

E-Cards Are Easy and Fun

2 Today, sending cards is easier and more fun than ever. You don't have to go to a store, buy a card, and send it in the mail. You don't even have to buy a stamp. Now, you can send an electronic card right from your computer at home. Electronic cards are fast, easy, and **inexpensive**. Many of them are even **free**. Some have sound, music, and pictures that move. You can type in your own **message**. You can even send electronic cards and postcards in many different languages.

A Popular E-Card Company

3 One popular electronic card company is called E-Cards. It was started in San Francisco in 1995. Since then, millions of cards have been sent by E-Cards. The owners of E-Cards care about the earth and nature. They give some of the money they make to groups that help save endangered[1] animals. They also want their cards to be **educational**. Many cards have pictures of endangered animals. When you click on the picture of the animal, you can read interesting information about it.

4 The next time you want to say "happy birthday," "happy new year," "congratulations," or "get well" to someone, try sending an electronic card. Or the next time you're on a vacation, send someone an e-postcard. It's a fast and fun way to say hello to friends and family while you're away.

[1] **endangered** – animals or plants which may soon not exist because there are very few now alive

After You Read

Comprehension Check

Read these statements. If a statement is true, write *T* on the line. If it is false, write *F*.

_____ 1. Postcards are not very popular.

_____ 2. You need a stamp to send an electronic card.

_____ 3. People send cards for many occasions.

_____ 4. Electronic cards are easy to send and receive.

_____ 5. The owners of E-Cards believe in helping nature and animals.

Vocabulary Practice

A Complete each sentence with the correct word.

educational	free	graduation
inexpensive	message	

1. Many e-cards don't cost any money. They are _____.

2. You can type your own _____ in most e-cards.

3. It is common to send _____ cards to people when they finish high school.

4. The owners of E-Cards want their customers to learn about animals. Their cards are _____.

5. Electronic cards are fast and _____.

B Circle the correct answer.

1. If you get something for <u>free</u>, you _____.
   a. don't pay for it
   b. pay a lot for it

2. Which is more <u>educational</u>?
   a. a history textbook
   b. a thank-you note

3. Which is an <u>inexpensive</u> gift?
   a. a new car
   b. a box of candy

4. Who would you send a <u>graduation</u> card to?

    a. someone who just got married

    b. someone who just finished high school

5. Which <u>message</u> would you write on a card for your sick friend?

    a. Get well soon!

    b. Have a good vacation!

✓ **Learning Synonyms and Antonyms**

C Decide if the following pairs of words are synonyms or antonyms. If they are synonyms, circle *S.* If they are antonyms, circle *A.*

1. easier	harder	S	A
2. expensive	inexpensive	S	A
3. message	note	S	A
4. event	occasion	S	A
5. free	expensive	S	A

Write a Message

Write a message for each e-card. Use the messages below, or make up your own.

Messages

Hope you get well soon.

Have a great trip!

Good luck in your new house.

Best wishes on your graduation day.

All my love on Valentine's Day.

Wishing you a very happy birthday.

Read a Calendar

Janet is going to send several e-cards in May. Scan her calendar to answer these questions.

1. What kind of e-card will Janet send to David? _____

2. On which day of the week will she send a Mother's Day e-card to her mother? _____

3. What kind of e-card will she send to Jane? _____

4. Who will she send an anniversary card to? _____

MAY						
Su	**M**	**Tu**	**W**	**Th**	**F**	**Sa**
				1	2 Go to doctor at 3:00 P.M.	3
4	5	6	7 Meeting at school, 7 P.M.	8	9	10
11 Mother's Day	12	13 Lunch with Keiko & Kumi	14	15	16 Sue and Ed's anniversary	17
18 Go to movie with Samuel	19	20	21 Jane's birthday	22	23 Rosa is visiting _____	24 _____
25 _____	26	27 David's graduation	28	29 Meeting with Mr. Sen	30	31

Easy Ways to Keep in Touch

Before You Read

A Discuss these questions with a partner.

1. Do you have any friends who live far away from you? How do you communicate with them? How often do you see them?
2. How many people do you consider your "best friends"? What are their names?

B Study these words and phrases from the reading. Write each word or phrase next to the correct definition.

hear from   lonely   lose touch with
make a commitment   make a habit of

1.	to get news or information from someone
2.	to promise to do something
3.	to stop having regular communication with someone
4.	unhappy because you are not with other people
5.	to do something often and regularly

EASY WAYS TO KEEP IN TOUCH

Ashley Stephens, Daily News *personal adviser*

Dear Adviser:

1 I moved to the United States two years ago for my work. I love my job, but I really miss my friends back home in Mexico City. I feel **lonely** without them. I see them when I go to Mexico, but I can't go very often. I feel like I am not part of their lives anymore. I don't want to **lose touch with** them. What should I do?

Sad Friend

Dear Sad Friend:

2 It is sad to lose touch with your friends. But you don't have to. There are lots of ways to keep in touch with them. You just need to **make a commitment** to do it.

3 The Internet makes it easy to communicate with your friends next door and around the world. Most of your friends probably have e-mail addresses. **Make a habit of** e-mailing them at least once a week. It's fun and inexpensive. If you don't have a computer at work or at home, go to the library. Most libraries have computers you can use for free. Or find an Internet café, where you can enjoy a cup of coffee while you write. It only takes a few minutes to e-mail, and your friends will be happy you did. And you'll be happy when they write back to you!

4 What about instant messaging? It's another great way to communicate with your friends online. With instant messaging, you can "talk" to many friends at the same time. Find a time when all your friends can be online together. When that happens, you'll feel like you are really part of the group again!

5 Remember that "a picture is worth a thousand words." Share photos with your friends. If you have a digital camera, send pictures to your friends over the Internet. If you don't have a digital camera, you can always send a photo by regular mail. You can also send text messages and pictures by cell phone. But don't forget about calling, too. Sometimes, just hearing a friend's voice will make you feel better.

6 Don't wait for the next holiday or special occasion to get in touch with your friends in Mexico. It doesn't matter whether you e-mail, call, or send a picture or card through the mail. Everyone likes to **hear from** friends. Our connections to one another are the most important things in our lives—don't lose touch with your friends!

Adviser

Comprehension Check

Check the statements that the adviser would agree with.

_____ 1. There are lots of ways to keep in touch with old friends.

_____ 2. E-mail messages are expensive to send.

_____ 3. Most libraries have computers you can use for free.

_____ 4. With instant messaging, you can only communicate with one person.

_____ 5. You can send text messages and pictures by cell phone.

_____ 6. It is a bad idea to send your friends photos.

_____ 7. You should never send letters in the mail.

_____ 8. Our connections to our friends are important.

Vocabulary Practice

71 percent of those who read advice columns are female. 56 percent of those who read advice columns are between the ages of 26 and 50.

A Complete each sentence with the correct word or phrase.

| hear from | lonely | lose touch with |
| make a commitment | make a habit of | |

1. It is sad to _____ your friends.

2. You should _____ to keep in touch with your friends.

3. Everyone likes to _____ their friends.

4. Do you feel sad and _____ when your friends are far away?

5. _____ calling your friends once a week.

B Cross out the word or phrase in each group that does not belong.

1. make a habit of	do often	make a guess
2. promise	commitment	question
3. lonely	happy	excited
4. hear from	lose touch with	get news from

Learning Expressions with *Make*

In this chapter, you learned the expressions *make a commitment* and *make a habit of.* There are many expressions in English that begin with *make.* Learning these expressions will help you expand your vocabulary and become a better reader.

C Match each expression with the correct definition. Work in a small group.

Expression	Definition
_____ 1. make a mistake	**a.** try hard
_____ 2. make sure	**b.** decide
_____ 3. make up your mind	**c.** be certain
_____ 4. make an effort	**d.** give a false reason
_____ 5. make an excuse	**e.** do something wrong

D Complete each sentence with the correct expression(s) from Exercise C.

1. If you really try and _____ to do your best, you probably won't _____.

2. Please _____ about where you want to eat dinner. We need to go soon.

3. I can't remember if I locked the car doors. Please _____ they are locked.

4. I know you can come to my party. Don't _____ this time!

Talk It Over

Discuss these questions as a class.

1. How important is it to you to keep in touch with old friends?
2. Do you have a digital camera? Do you e-mail pictures to people?
3. Do you send text messages or instant messages to people? How often?
4. What other ways can you think of to keep in touch with old friends?

Write a Response

Read this letter to an adviser. Then write your own response. Try to use at least three expressions with *make.* Compare responses with a partner.

New ▾ Reply Reply All Forward Flag ▾ Print Delete ▾

Dear Adviser:

My best friend moved to Tokyo last month to teach English. She will be gone for at least two years. I am afraid she will make many new friends and forget about me. What can I do to help her remember me?

Needs Help

Dear Needs Help:

_____

_____

_____

_____

_____

_____

Sending Cyber-Hugs

Before You Read

A Discuss these questions with a partner.

1. Do people hug one another in your culture? Do you think it is important for parents to hug their children?
2. The Internet has changed our lives in many ways. How has it changed your life? Give some examples.
3. How often do you use the Internet? What do you use it for?

B Study these words and phrases from the article. Write each word or phrase next to the correct definition.

control   figured out   put on
technology   useful

1.	helping you do something
2.	to cover part of your body with clothes, shoes, etc.
3.	to make something do what you want
4.	knowledge, machines, and methods used in science and industry
5.	understood something after thinking about it

Sending Cyber-Hugs

1   Computers and the Internet have changed the way we communicate with other people. You can use the Internet to send e-mail messages for people to read. You can also use the Internet to send photos for people to see or music for them to hear. Today, the Internet uses only two of our senses[1]: sight and hearing. But all that could change in the near future. Soon you may be able to send people hugs that they can feel!

2   Scientists in Singapore discovered a way to send the sense of touch over the Internet. They hope the new **technology** will help parents keep in touch with their children. They think it will soon be possible for parents to hug their children using the Internet.

3   James Teh is a scientist at Nanyang Technological University in Singapore. He has already **figured out** a way for people to "touch" their pets over the Internet. To do this, Teh invented a wireless[2] "hug suit" for pets to wear. When people are far away from their pets, they can use a computer to **control** the hug suit. The suit gives the animal the feeling of being touched by its owner.

4   Now, Teh plans to use the same technology to make a hug suit for children. A child wearing the hug suit will be able to get

techshout.com

electronic hugs from his or her parents. Parents will use a computer to control the hug suit so the child feels like he or she is getting a hug. When parents **put on** a similar suit, they can be "hugged" back by their child.

5   Teh works with Professor Adrian Cheok. Cheok said, "These days, parents go on a lot of business trips, but with children, hugging and touching are very important." He thinks the new technology will be **useful** for parents and children. He believes that many people will want to use this new technology. What do *you* think?

---

[1] **senses** – the body's natural abilities to hear, see, taste, feel, and smell
[2] **wireless** – without wires

After You Read

A Check the topics discussed in the article.

❏ 1. where the hug suit was invented

❏ 2. how much a hug suit costs

❏ 3. why parents might like to use the hug suit

❏ 4. who invented the hug suit

❏ 5. what colors of hug suit will be for sale

❏ 6. using the hug suit for animals

B Read these statements. If a statement is true, write *T* on the line. If it is false, write *F*.

_____ 1. Computers and the Internet have changed our lives in many ways.

_____ 2. The Internet uses all five of our senses.

_____ 3. Scientists in Singapore found a way to send the sense of touch over the Internet.

_____ 4. James Teh has already made a hug suit for pets.

_____ 5. People must be near their pets to touch them over the Internet.

_____ 6. James Teh made a hug suit for children last year.

_____ 7. Professor Cheok thinks parents will want to use the new technology.

Vocabulary Practice

A Complete each sentence with the correct word or phrase.

control   figured out   put on
technology   useful

1. A person can _____ her pet's hug suit using the Internet.

2. Scientists hope the new _____ will help parents keep in touch with their children.

3. The scientists _____ how to send the sense of touch over the Internet.

4. Cheok thinks the hug suit will be _____ for parents and children.

5. A child must _____ a hug suit to get a hug over the Internet.

B Circle the correct answer.

1. When would you <u>put on</u> a coat?

    a. on a cold day

    b. on a hot day

2. If information is <u>useful</u>, it _____.

    a. helps you

    b. doesn't help you

3. When you <u>figure out</u> the meaning of a word, you _____.

    a. don't understand what it means

    b. understand what it means

4. Which is an example of new <u>technology</u>?

    a. cell phones that take pictures

    b. black-and-white television

5. When you <u>control</u> the volume on your radio, you _____.

    a. make the sound louder or softer

    b. turn the radio on or off

SKILL
FOR
SUCCESS

Learning Phrasal Verbs with *Put*

In this chapter, you learned the meaning of *put on*. *Put on* is a **phrasal verb**. Phrasal verbs usually have two parts: a verb and a preposition. The meaning of a phrasal verb is different from the meaning of its parts.

C Study these common phrasal verbs with *put.* Then complete each sentence with the correct verb.

put away—to put something in the place where it is usually kept

put down—to say bad things about someone or something

put off—to wait to do something, or to delay doing something

put out—to stop something, such as a fire or cigarette, from burning

1. You need to _____ the fire before you leave the campsite.

2. Please _____ all these toys before you go to sleep.

3. It's not very nice to _____ your little brother. It makes him feel sad.

4. Do some of your homework now. It's not a good idea to _____ everything until tomorrow.

Talk It Over

Discuss these questions as a class.

1. Do you think hug suits are a useful invention? Why or why not?
2. Do you think parents and children will send cyber-hugs? Why or why not?
3. Do you think people should spend time and money on this type of technology? Why or why not?

Improve Your Reading Speed

Circle the word in each row that is <u>different</u> from all the other words. Work as fast as you can.

1. when	then	when	when	when	when	when
2. yours	yours	yours	yours	years	yours	yours
3. new	new	now	new	new	new	new
4. our	our	our	our	out	our	our
5. there	these	there	there	there	there	there
6. much	much	muck	much	much	much	much
7. hug	hug	hug	hog	hug	hug	hug
8. my	may	my	my	my	my	my
9. him	him	his	him	him	him	him
10. ever	ever	ever	over	ever	ever	ever

Tie It All Together

Discussion

Discuss these questions in a small group.

1. What qualities do you think are important in a friend?
2. A popular English saying is, "A friend in need is a friend indeed." Do you agree or disagree? Why?
3. How does technology help you stay in touch with your friends and family?

Just for Fun

A Write a word to complete each sentence. Use one letter for each space. Then follow the directions below to solve the puzzle.

1. You shouldn't _f_ _o_ _r_ _g_ _e_ _t_ your old friends.
2. You need a _ _O__O_ _ _ _ _O_ _ _ to send and receive e-mail.
3. Scientists in _ _ _ _ _O__O_ _ _ _ want to send hugs over the Internet.
4. Most cities and towns have a cyber café where people can use the _ _O_ _ _O_ _ _ _.
5. With a _ _O_ _ _ _ _ _ camera, you can use the Internet to send pictures.

B Now, write the nine circled letters below. Then unscramble them to find a word about friends.

_t_ _ _ _ _ _ _ _ _

Friends are _____.

abcNEWS
Video Activity

Communication through the Ages
You will see a video about the history of long-distance communication. How do you think people kept in touch long ago?

A Study these words. Then watch the video.

device   drum   method

B Read this list of developments in communication and then watch the video again. Match each development with the correct time when it happened.

_____ 1. The Internet was first used.

_____ 2. Morse Code was created.

_____ 3. People used drums to communicate.

_____ 4. The Pony Express was used.

_____ 5. Telephone communication began.

a. In the 1870s

b. Thousands of years ago

c. In the 1960s

d. In 1837

e. In the mid-1800s

C Discuss these questions with a partner or in a small group.

1. Do you know of other kinds of communication people used in the past? When were they used? Who used them?

2. What are some disadvantages of communication today? Can you think of any ways to improve modern communication?

Reader's Journal   Think about the topics and ideas you have read about and discussed in this unit. Choose a topic from the list and write about it for ten to twenty minutes. Pick a topic from the following list, or choose one at your own.

- your best friend
- ways to stay in touch with friends
- why your friends are important to you

Vocabulary Self-Test

Complete each sentence with the correct word or phrase.

A control   educational   lose touch with
       message   technology

1. You can _____ your car better when you drive slowly.

2. _____ is changing the way we live.

3. I hope I don't _____ my old friends when I move.

4. The shows on Channel 7 are usually _____ shows.
   I watch them to learn new things.

5. You have a text _____ from Brigitte.

B graduation   hear from   inexpensive
       make a habit of   useful

1. A computer is _____ for doing homework.

2. The red jacket is _____. I have enough money to buy it.

3. You should _____ doing nice things for your friends.

4. Do you ever _____ Rafael? How is he?

5. Miriam started her nursing job a month after _____.

C figure out   free   lonely
       make a commitment   put on

1. The tickets to tonight's concert at the City Center are
   _____.

2. I felt _____ when my wife went away for a week.

3. If you have children, you must _____ to take care of
   them.

4. I couldn't _____ how to do my math homework.

5. Aya _____ her best dress for the party.

THE WORK WORLD

Work is a big part of life for most people. Some people are lucky enough to enjoy their work. In this unit, you will read about three people who have very different types of jobs but who really enjoy what they do.

Points to Ponder

Look at the pictures above and discuss these questions in a small group.

1. Where do these people work?

2. What are their jobs?

3. Would you like to have any of these jobs? Why or why not?

What's New?

Before You Read

A Discuss these questions with a partner.

1. Are you interested in clothing styles? Where do you find out about new styles? Watching TV? Reading magazines? Watching people?
2. Do you care about wearing clothes that are stylish or popular? Why or why not?
3. Look at your classmates' clothes. What colors are popular?

B Study these words from the article. Write each word next to the correct definition.

fashionable   forecast   interviews

jewelry   occupation   report

1.	a person's job
2.	things such as rings and necklaces that you wear on your body
3.	to say what you think will happen in the future
4.	popular at a particular time; in style
5.	asks someone questions
6.	a piece of writing that gives people information

Reading with a Purpose段
✓ **Reading with a Purpose**
C You are going to read about a woman whose job is to make predictions about fashion. What are three things you hope to learn from the article?

1. _____

2. _____

3. _____

What's New?

1 Many people would love to have Lisa Cohen's job. Every day, she watches television and music videos. She reads newspapers and magazines. Sometimes, she goes to a movie, a store, or a different city to watch people. She wants to see what is **fashionable** and popular. Lisa has to do these things for her job.

2 Lisa's job is to try to understand what is fashionable and popular now and to predict, or **forecast**, what will be fashionable and popular in the future. How does Lisa do this? She looks closely at the clothes people wear.

She also observes their hair, makeup[1], and **jewelry.** Sometimes, she **interviews** people on the street about what they like. She asks them questions about the kinds of things they buy and wear. Other times, she brings a group of people to her office. They talk about which fashions they like and don't like.

3 When Lisa has enough information, she writes a **report**. Companies want the information in her reports. The information helps them make products that people will like and want to buy. For example, one year Lisa predicted that red would be a popular color. As a result, clothing companies made lots of red clothing. It was easy to find red shoes, red scarves, red coats, red nail polish, red skirts, and red sweaters in all the stores.

4 Lisa likes her job because she meets interesting people and goes to interesting places. She thinks being a fashion forecaster is a great **occupation**. She says there is only one problem with her job: She must always look fashionable, too!

[1] **makeup –**

Chapter 1   **69**

After You Read

A Check the things that Lisa does for her job.

❑ 1. read magazines

❑ 2. make predictions about fashion

❑ 3. make clothes

❑ 4. observe what people wear

❑ 5. sell makeup

❑ 6. observe peoples' hair and jewelry

❑ 7. write reports

B Read these statements. If a statement is true, write *T* on the line. If it is false, write *F.*

_____ 1. Lisa doesn't have to watch television for her job.

_____ 2. Lisa goes to interesting places for her job.

_____ 3. Lisa predicted that blue would be a popular color.

_____ 4. Lisa meets interesting people in her job.

_____ 5. Lisa must look fashionable for her job.

A Write the correct word to replace each underlined word or phrase.

fashionable	forecast	interviews
jewelry	occupation	report

1. Lisa thinks being a fashion forecaster is a great <u>job</u>. _____

2. Lisa watches people to see what is <u>in style</u>. _____

3. She looks at their clothes, hair, and <u>rings and necklaces</u>.

_____

4. Sometimes Lisa <u>asks questions to</u> people on the street about what

they like. _____

5. Then she writes a <u>description with information</u> for companies to use.

_____

6. Lisa has to <u>predict</u> what will be fashionable and popular in the future.

_____

B Circle the correct answer.

1. Where would you read about the kind of clothes that are fashionable now?
   a. in magazines
   b. in textbooks

2. For which occupation would a person need to go to college?
   a. doctor
   b. taxi driver

3. What do you do when someone interviews you?
   a. write letters to that person
   b. answer that person's questions

4. What do you need in order to write a report?
   a. information
   b. clothes

5. Which is an example of jewelry?
   a. a ring
   b. a coat

6. What is something you would forecast?
   a. tomorrow's weather
   b. the invention of the Internet

✓**Learning Synonyms**

C Use the list below to write the correct synonym for each word from the article.

job   looks at   predict   questions   stylish

Word	Synonym
fashionable	1.
forecast	2.
observes	3.
interviews	4.
occupation	5.

D Complete the paragraph with the synonyms from the chart in Exercise C.

Lisa has a _____ in the fashion business. She is a fashion
                    1.

forecaster. How does she _____ what is going to be
                               2.

_____ in the future? She _____ what people
   3.   4.

are wearing. She reads magazines, watches TV, and goes to the movies.

She also _____ people about what they like and dislike.
            5.

✓ **Organizing Words**

E Lisa observes the things people wear, such as their clothes, makeup, and jewelry. Read the list of words below. Organize the words by writing each one in the correct column. Use your dictionary to help you.

blush	boots	bracelet	earrings	eye shadow
jeans	lipstick	nail polish	necklace	pants
ring	sandals	shoes	shorts	skirt
slippers	sneakers	suit	sweater	T-shirt

Clothing	Footwear	Jewelry	Makeup

Talk It Over

Discuss these questions as a class.

1. Would you like to have Lisa's job? Why or why not?
2. Are there any occupations in the fashion business that you are interested in? Which ones?
3. Do you think people care too much about trying to be fashionable? Why or why not?

Take a Survey

A survey is a list of questions you ask people in order to find out about their opinions and behaviors. You will take a survey to learn about your classmates' thoughts about fashion.

Interview five of your classmates. Ask them to answer the three questions in the chart. Share your survey results with your classmates.

Classmates Name	Do you read fashion magazines?	Do you care about wearing clothes that are in style?	What color do you think will be fashionable next year?

A Job Change

Before You Read

A Discuss these questions with a partner.

1. How often do people in your country change jobs?
2. Do you like sports? Which ones?
3. Have you ever gone mountain climbing? Did you enjoy it?

B Study these words and phrases from the article. Write each word or phrase next to the correct definition.

adventure   boss   challenge

earn   successful   take a break

1.	to stop doing something for a short time
2.	a person who tells other people what work to do
3.	an exciting activity
4.	having a good result; popular
5.	something difficult that tests your ability
6.	to get something, usually money, for doing work

Skimming for the Main Idea

Most reading passages have one **main idea**. **Skimming** is a way to read a passage quickly to find the main idea. When you skim, do not read every word or stop to look up words you do not know in a dictionary. Just read as fast as you can to find the main idea.

C Skim the article one time. Then choose the statement you think describes the main idea.

1. Teaching science is not an exciting job.
2. A. J. LaFleur changed his job.
3. A. J. thinks mountain climbing is exciting.

A JOB CHANGE

1 Today, A. J. LaFleur is a **successful** businessman. But he wasn't always a businessman. He was once a teacher. He taught science to high school students for many years. For a long time, A. J. enjoyed teaching. He liked his students, and they liked him. He did a good job at his school. Then he got bored. He wanted to **take a break** from teaching. He wanted to try something new and exciting. So he decided to take a trip to Nepal and climb mountains. Mountain climbing was a **challenge.** It was also a great **adventure.**

2 The next year, A. J. was in the classroom teaching science again. But teaching wasn't exciting anymore. He wasn't learning very much. It was a good job, but A. J. wanted something more. He wanted a new job. What could he do? He thought about what kind of job he would like. Finally, he decided to open a store. He named the store The Mountain Goat.

3 The Mountain Goat is a special kind of store. It sells clothes and equipment[1] for outdoor sports like mountain climbing. You can buy skis, maps, tents, boots, and lots of other things at The Mountain Goat.

4 Opening a store was A. J's first job as a businessman. He was worried but excited. Could he **earn** enough money for his family? A. J. worked very hard. He was a good businessman, and he understood what his customers needed. He was happy because every day was a challenge. He liked the hard work, and his business was successful. And there was always something new to learn. "You can't fall asleep!" he said.

5 Today, A. J. likes being the **boss.** Now he has three stores and a website. He has an assistant[2], and he can take vacations when he wants. He is already planning his next trip. He's going mountain climbing in Tibet!

[1] **equipment** – the things that you need for an activity

[2] **assistant** – someone who helps a person in his or her job

After You Read

A Read these statements. If a statement is true, write *T* on the line. If it is false, write *F.*

_____ 1. A. J. never enjoyed teaching science.

_____ 2. A. J. teaches business at a new school.

_____ 3. The Mountain Goat is a successful business.

_____ 4. A. J. is too busy to take vacations now.

B Circle the correct answer.

1. A. J. used to be a _____ teacher.
   a. business
   b. science
   c. mountain-climbing

2. Now, A. J. has his own _____.
   a. school
   b. mountain
   c. business

3. The Mountain Goat sells _____ for outdoor sports.
   a. clothes
   b. stores
   c. jobs

4. A. J. was worried about _____ when he opened his store.
   a. earning enough money
   b. going mountain climbing
   c. teaching science

5. A. J. is going to _____ on his next vacation.
   a. climb a mountain in Tibet
   b. open a store in Nepal
   c. sell sports equipment

Vocabulary Practice

A Complete each sentence with the correct word(s) or phrase.

adventure	boss	challenge
earn	successful	take a break

1. A. J.'s store was _____. He was a good businessman.

2. Mountain climbing can be difficult. It is a _____. It is also very exciting. That makes it an _____.

3. A. J. wanted to stop teaching for a short time, so he decided to _____.

4. At first, A. J. was worried that he might not _____ enough money for his family.

5. A. J. has his own store. He likes being the _____.

B Circle the correct answer.

1. When you take a break, you _____.
   a. stop doing something for a short time
   b. work very hard for ten minutes

2. If you are the boss, you _____.
   a. tell other people what to do
   b. do what other people tell you

3. A successful business _____.
   a. loses money
   b. makes money

4. When something is a great adventure, it is _____.
   a. fun and exciting
   b. old and boring

5. _____ is a challenge for most people.
   a. Looking at a mountain
   b. Climbing to the top of a mountain

SKILL FOR SUCCESS

Understanding Word Parts: The Suffix *-er*

The suffix *-er* is added to a word to mean *someone who does something*. For example, in this chapter, you learned that A. J. was a teacher and mountain climber. A teacher is someone who teaches. A mountain climber is someone who climbs mountains.

C Complete each sentence with the correct word ending in *-er.*

baker   driver   runner   writer

1. Someone who writes is a _____.

2. A person who drives a bus is a bus _____.

3. A person who runs is a _____.

4. Someone who bakes is a _____.

SKILL FOR SUCCESS

Learning Expressions with *Take*

In this chapter, you learned the expression *take a break.* There are many expressions in English that begin with *take.* Learning these expressions will help you expand your vocabulary and become a better reader.

D Match each expression with the correct definition. Work in a small group.

Expression	Definition
_____ 1. take up	a. rest
_____ 2. take it easy	b. spend as much time as you need to do something right
_____ 3. take your word for it	
_____ 4. take care of	c. begin to do
_____ 5. take your time	d. believe what you say
	e. do the work or make the plans for something

E Complete the conversation with the expressions from Exercise D.

A: Do you want to go to a movie tonight?

B: Sure. I've been studying all day. I want to _____ this
   1.
   evening.

A: What do you want to see?

B: How about *The City of Stars*? It's a new movie about a teacher who
   decides to _____ space travel. I heard it's an exciting
                2.
   movie. I think you'll like it.

A: OK. I'll _____.
             3.

B: Let's meet at the theater at 7:00. I've got to finish my homework first.

A: That's fine. _____. It's only 4:00 now.
                4.

B: Can you get the tickets in advance?

A: Sure. Don't worry. I'll _____ it.
                            5.

Talk It Over

Discuss these questions as a class.

1. Would you like to teach? What would you want to teach?
2. Would you like to own a store? What kind of store? What would you sell?

Scan the help-wanted ads below to answer these questions.

1. Who should you call if you are interested in the English teacher job?

   _____

2. How much money does a part-time driver for Pizza Palace make an hour? _____

3. To which company should you apply if you want a job as a full-time secretary? _____

4. What number should you call to apply for a job as a delivery person?

   _____

5. How much experience is needed to teach at the English Language Academy? _____

6. What skills are needed to be a secretary at Computer Corner?

   _____

HELP WANTED

SECRETARY NEEDED

Computer Corner is looking for a full-time secretary.

Must have excellent telephone and computer skills.

Apply at: 312 Jefferson Avenue, or e-mail Paul@ccorner.net

HELP WANTED

LOOKING FOR ENGLISH TEACHER

English Language Academy is looking for a

   full-time English teacher.

Must have at least 3 years' experience.

Call Dr. Baker if interested.

267-555-3478, ext. 212

HELP WANTED

DELIVERY PERSON WANTED

Part-time. Driver's license required.

Must be able to work evenings and weekends. $6.50/hour

Call Ronnie at Pizza Palace: 809-555-7000

A Popular Cartoonist

© 1998 Randy Glasbergen.   www.glasbergen.com

Before You Read

A Discuss these questions with a partner.

1. Look at the cartoon above. Do you think it is funny? Why or why not?
2. Do you like to read cartoons? Why or why not?
3. Do you read cartoons in the newspaper? In magazines? On the Internet?

B Study these words and phrases from the interview. Write each word or phrase next to the correct definition.

career   continued   disappoint
draw   for a living

1.	to make a picture using a pencil or pen
2.	kept doing without stopping
3.	in order to earn money
4.	a job that you know a lot about and do for a long time
5.	to make someone unhappy because something is not as good as he or she wanted it to be

✓ **Reading with a Purpose**

C You are going to read an interview with a man whose job is to create cartoons. What are three things you hope to learn from the interview?

1. _____

2. _____

3. _____

A Popular Cartoonist

1   Randy Glasbergen creates cartoons **for a living**. He is one of America's most popular cartoonists. His most famous cartoon series is called *The Better Half*. You can see *The Better Half* in newspapers around the world. Randy also creates cartoons for the Internet.

2   **Interviewer:** When did you start to **draw** cartoons?

Randy Glasbergen: I started to draw cartoons when I was a child, just for fun. When I was in high school, I sent some of my cartoons to magazines. I was surprised when a few magazines began to buy and publish[1] my cartoons. In college, I **continued** to write and sell cartoons. More and more magazines bought them. Over the years, my **career** as a cartoonist slowly grew. By 1982, my cartoons were in many

[1] **publish** – to print and sell something, such as a book, newspaper, or magazine

newspapers. In 1995, I started my daily Internet cartoon.

3 **I:** Did you ever study art?

RG: No. I have no formal art or cartooning education. I just learned by studying the work of others and practicing, practicing, practicing.

4 **I:** Where do you get the ideas for your cartoons?

RG: I get my ideas from things I hear, read, or see on TV. I try to write about things that are important to people. People care about their own lives, families, jobs, and pets. So that's what I write about. For most cartoonists, the idea comes before the drawing. A good cartoonist is not an artist who can also write. A good cartoonist is a writer who can also draw.

5 **I:** What helped you become so successful?

RG: That's easy. The Internet. It has really helped my career grow. Most of my new readers find my cartoons on the Internet. Thanks to the Internet, my work is published all over the world. You can see my cartoons in lots of magazines and newspapers. If you want to start a career in the cartoon business, the Internet is the best way.

6 **I:** Do you have a Web site?

RG: Yes. You can see a new cartoon every day on my website at www.glasbergen.com. You can also buy cards, shirts, calendars, and other things with my cartoons printed on them. People in businesses order cartoons from my Web site, too. Sometimes they use them in reports.

7 **I:** What is your goal for your work?

RG: My main goal is to write something funny that people will want to read each day. I don't want to **disappoint** my readers. If one of my cartoons is put up on a wall or a refrigerator door, I know it's a success. ■

After You Read

Comprehension Check

A Check the topics that Randy talks about in the interview.

❑ 1. when he began drawing cartoons

❑ 2. his favorite books and movies

❑ 3. where he gets his ideas for cartoons

❑ 4. what he learned in school

❑ 5. how the Internet helped him

❑ 6. what he plans to write about in the future

❑ 7. what his website offers

❑ 8. his main goal

B Read these statements. If a statement is true, write *T* on the line. If it is false, write *F*.

_____ 1. Randy started drawing cartoons when he was a child.

_____ 2. Randy was surprised when some magazines bought his cartoons.

_____ 3. Randy stopped writing cartoons when he was in college.

_____ 4. You can see a new cartoon every day on Randy's Web site.

C Circle the correct answer.

1. What helped Randy become successful?

   a. newspapers

   b. the Internet

   c. magazines

2. Where does Randy get the ideas for his cartoons?

   a. from other cartoons he reads in magazines

   b. from things he hears, reads, or sees on TV

   c. from websites on the Internet

3. Why do businesses order cartoons from Randy's Web site?

   a. to use in reports

   b. to sell to newspapers

   c. to find new customers

4. When did Randy start his daily Internet cartoon?

   a. in 1982

   b. in 1995

   c. when he was a child

Vocabulary Practice

A Complete each sentence with the correct word or phrase.

career	continued	disappoint
draw	for a living	

1. Randy earns money selling his cartoons. He creates cartoons

   _____ .

2. Randy started to _____ cartoons when he was a child.

3. In college, Randy _____ to sell cartoons.

4. Over the years, Randy's _____ as a cartoonist grew.

5. He wants his readers to enjoy reading his cartoons. He doesn't want to

   _____ them.

B Circle the correct answer.

1. Which would you use to <u>draw</u> with?
   a. a pencil
   b. a magazine

2. Which is an example of a <u>career</u> in education?
   a. a teacher
   b. a doctor

3. If you <u>disappoint</u> someone, he or she is _____ .
   a. happy
   b. unhappy

4. If you do something <u>for a living</u>, you _____ .
   a. get money to do it
   b. pay money to do it

5. If you <u>continued</u> watching a program on TV, you _____ .
   a. stopped watching it
   b. kept watching it

SKILL FOR SUCCESS

Understanding Word Parts: The Suffix *-ist*

The suffix *-ist* is added to a word to mean *someone who does something*. In this chapter, you learned that Randy is a cartoonist, or someone who makes cartoons.

C Complete each sentence with the correct word ending in *-ist*.

artist   scientist   typist   violinist

1. Someone who plays the violin is a _____.

2. A person who makes art is an _____.

3. A person who studies science is a _____.

4. Someone who types is a _____.

Take a Survey

Interview three of your classmates. Ask them to tell you three qualities they think are important for each job. Complete the chart with their answers. Use the words from the list or other words that you know. Share your survey results with your classmates.

brave   careful   creative   friendly
honest   intelligent   kind   lucky
organized   polite   responsible   strong

Job	Classmate's Name: _____	Classmate's Name: _____	Classmate's Name: _____
teacher	1. 2. 3.	1. 2. 3.	1. 2. 3.
businessperson	1. 2. 3.	1. 2. 3.	1. 2. 3.
firefighter	1. 2. 3.	1. 2. 3.	1. 2. 3.
cartoonist	1. 2. 3.	1. 2. 3.	1. 2. 3.

Discussion

Discuss these questions in a small group.

1. What jobs do you think would be boring? Exciting? Dangerous?
2. Which do you prefer, working inside or working outside? Why?
3. What are the three most interesting jobs you can think of?

Just for Fun

Complete the crossword puzzle with words from the unit.

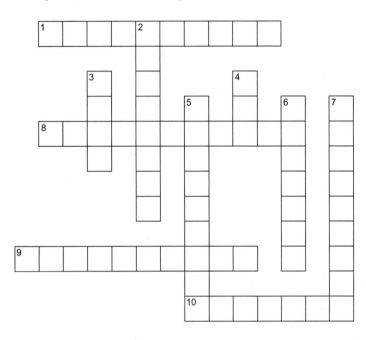

Across

1. to do the work or make the plans for something (3 words)

8. popular; in style

9. someone who draws cartoons

10. You can find Randy Glasbergen's cartoons on his _____.

Down

2. to keep doing something without stopping

3. A. J. La Fleur is the _____ at The Mountain Goat.

4. an occupation

5. to ask questions

6. A ring is a type of _____.

7. Climbing mountains is an _____.

Human Cannonball

This video is about a man who has a very unusual job in a circus. Have you ever been to a circus? What do people do or see there?

A Study these words and phrases. Then watch the video.

cannon(ball)   free time   thrill

B Read these questions and then watch the video again. Match each question with the correct answer.

_____ 1. What does Thomas do in the circus?

_____ 2. How many times a day does Thomas perform?

_____ 3. How fast does he travel through the air?

_____ 4. How much does Thomas earn at his job?

_____ 5. What part of his job does Thomas not like?

a. the pain

b. get shot out of a cannon

c. $25,000

d. twice

e. 55 miles per hour

C Discuss these questions with a partner or in a small group.

1. Would you do a job that was dangerous or painful? Why or why not?
2. Sean Thomas travels to many new towns for his work. Would you enjoy traveling for a job? Why or why not?

Reader's Journal   Think about the topics and ideas you have read about and discussed in this unit. Choose a topic from the list and write about it for ten to twenty minutes. Pick a topic from the following list, or choose one of your own.

• the career you would like to have
• the best or worst job you have ever had
• what jobs will be like in the future

Vocabulary Self-Test

Complete each sentence with the correct word or phrase.

A adventure   disappoint   fashionable
for a living   jewelry   successful

1. I hate to _____ you, but we have to cancel our vacation.

2. Shawn has an interesting job. He teaches English _____.

3. My mother started her business ten years ago. Today, she is a _____ businesswoman.

4. Our trip to Nepal was very exciting. It was an _____.

5. Caesar designs _____ women's clothes.

6. Magdalena's husband buys her beautiful _____.

B boss   draw   earns
forecasted   occupation   report

1. Naoko had to write a ten-page _____ for her history class.

2. The newspaper _____ snow for today, but it didn't snow.

3. Norman _____ extra money by working in a restaurant on weekends.

4. I had to write my name and _____ on the form.

5. Our _____ usually lets us leave work early on Friday afternoons.

6. My daughter likes to _____ pictures.

C career   challenge   continued
interviewed   take a break

1. Don had a long and happy _____ as a doctor.

2. Hajime thought the computer course would be easy, but he found it to be a _____.

3. Natalia _____ to work after she had the baby.

4. I usually _____ from studying at about 8:00.

5. Alicia _____ her grandfather about his childhood.

LANGUAGE AND LIFE

Did you know there are more than 5,000 languages spoken in the world today? Learning a new language can be difficult. But it also can be fun. In this unit, you will learn interesting things about the languages of the world.

Points to Ponder

Discuss these questions in a small group.

1. What is your native language (the language you grew up speaking)?

2. How many languages do you speak?

3. How do you say *hello* in your native language? Teach your group how to say *hello* in your language.

Languages of the World

Before You Read

A Discuss these questions with a partner.

1. Why are you studying English?
2. What other languages would you like to learn?
3. Do you think your native language is hard to learn? Why or why not?

B Study these words from the article. Write each word next to the correct definition.

disappears   enormous   equal

express   simple

1.	easy to learn or understand
2.	having the same amount or level
3.	very big
4.	stops existing or being
5.	to say or do something to let people know what you think or how you feel

✓ Thinking about What You Know

C You are going to read an article about languages. Check the statements you think are true about languages.

❏ 1. There are more than 5,000 languages in the world.

❏ 2. Many of the world's languages are dying.

❏ 3. The first language began 1,000 years ago.

❏ 4. The English language has a very large number of words.

❏ 5. Some English words come from other languages.

❏ 6. Some languages are easy to learn.

❏ 7. More people speak Chinese than any other language.

✓ Predicting

D Follow these steps to make predictions about the article on page 94.

1. Think about the title. Write it on the line.

   _____

2. Read the four headings. Write them on the lines.

   _____

   _____

   _____

   _____

3. Look at the charts. What information is in the first chart?

   _____

   What information is in the second chart?

   _____

4. Check the ideas you think will be discussed in the article.

   ❏ a. the number of languages in the world today

   ❏ b. how to learn Chinese

   ❏ c. information about the English vocabulary

   ❏ d. languages that are dying

   ❏ e. words in the English language

Languages of the World

1 Many thousands of years ago, people slowly started to use spoken language. Scientists do not know exactly when, where, or why human language began.

One World, Many Languages

2 Today, there are 5,000 to 6,000 different languages. Mandarin Chinese is the most common language. More than a billion people speak Mandarin. The other most common languages are English, Hindustani, Spanish, Russian, and Arabic. In some parts of the world, many different languages are spoken in one place. For example, together the 5.5 million people living on the island of Papua New Guinea speak more than 800 languages.

All Languages Are Equal

3 Some languages may seem **simple**. Other languages may seem difficult. But languages are actually **equal**. No language is simpler or more difficult than any other language. Each language has sounds and words so that its speakers can talk about anything they want. Every language can also make new words to **express** new ideas. So it is no surprise that all languages change through time.

Languages Are Dying

4 Many of world's languages are dying. One language **disappears** about every two weeks. Only older people speak these languages. Children cannot speak them. This is the first step in the death of a language. Today,

Most Common Languages	Number of Speakers
1. Chinese (Mandarin)	1,075,000,000
2. English	514,000,000
3. Hindustani	496,000,000
4. Spanish	425,000,000
5. Russian	275,000,000
6. Arabic	256,000,000
7. Bengali	215,000,000
8. Portuguese	194,000,000
9. Malay-Indonesian	176,000,000
10. French	129,000,000

there are 2,000 languages that have only 1,000 speakers each. Australian languages are a good example of this. There are about 200 Australian languages, but most of them have only about ten speakers. Twelve Australian languages have only one speaker.

English Word	Original Language
pizza	Italian
hotel	French
yogurt	Turkish
sofa	Arabic
shampoo	Hindustani
window	Icelandic

The Huge English Vocabulary

5 The English language is changing, too. But it's not dying; it's growing. English has an **enormous** vocabulary. Eighty percent of English words come from other languages.

Whenever English speakers meet people from other cultures, they borrow[1] some of their words. Here are some English words that come from other languages. ■

[1] **borrow** – to use something that is not yours

After You Read

Comprehension Check

A Read these statements. If a statement is true, write *T* on the line. If it is false, write *F*.

_____ 1. Human language began very quickly.

_____ 2. There are thousands of languages today.

_____ 3. Mandarin Chinese is the most common language today.

_____ 4. Some languages are simpler than others.

_____ 5. All languages change.

_____ 6. Many of the world's languages are disappearing.

_____ 7. Only a few English words come from other languages.

✓ **Scanning for Information**

B Scan the article to find the number that answers each question.

1. How many different languages are there in the world today? _____

2. How many languages have only 1,000 speakers? _____

3. What percentage of English words come from other languages? _____

4. What is the population of Papua New Guinea? _____

5. How many Australian languages are there today? _____

6. How many Australian languages have only one speaker? _____

7. How many people speak Mandarin? _____

F Y I
Half of the languages spoken today will die in the next 100 years.

Vocabulary Practice

A Complete each sentence with the correct word.

disappears   enormous   equal
express   simple

1. One language _____ every two weeks.

2. All languages can make new words to _____ new ideas.

3. It is not true that some languages are _____ and others are difficult. All languages are _____ in difficulty.

4. The English language has a lot of words. It has an _____ vocabulary.

B Circle the correct answer.

1. If the instructions for making something are <u>simple</u>, they are _____.

   a. hard to follow

   b. easy to follow

Before there were written languages, there were probably 10,000 to 15,000 spoken languages.

2. If two people are <u>equal</u> in height, _____.

   a. they are the same height

   b. one person is taller

3. What happens when a language <u>disappears</u>?

   a. No one speaks it anymore.

   b. Lots of people still speak it.

4. If a language has an <u>enormous</u> vocabulary, it has _____.

   a. a huge number of words

   b. a normal number of words

5. If you want to <u>express</u> that you are happy, you should _____.

   a. eat

   b. smile

C Cross out the word in each group that does not belong.

1. simple   difficult   easy

2. enormous   small   huge

3. express   sleep   communicate

4. different   equal   same

SKILL FOR SUCCESS

Understanding Word Parts: The Prefix *dis-*
A **prefix** is a letter or group of letters added to the beginning of a word to form another word. **The prefix *dis-*** changes a word into its opposite. For example, *dishonest* means *not honest.*

D Circle the correct word or phrase to complete each sentence. Use your dictionary to help you.

1. Jason doesn't like cats. He (likes /(dislikes) them.
2. My brother and I like to do the same things. We usually (agree / disagree) about what to do on the weekends.
3. Marsha always tells the truth. I usually (believe / disbelieve) what she says.
4. I don't think people should talk on their cell phones in restaurants. I (approve / disapprove) of it.

Talk It Over

Discuss these questions as a class.

1. Do you think English is difficult to learn? Why or why not?
2. What words in your language come from other languages?
3. Do any English words come from your language? Which ones?

Hangul Day

Before You Read

A Discuss these questions with a partner.

1. Does your language have an alphabet? How many letters does it have?
2. Can most people in your country read and write?
3. Is it easy or difficult to learn to write in your language? Why?

B Study these words from the article. Write each word next to the correct definition.

ceremonies   contests   foolish

honor   wise

1.	competitions for a prize
2.	not intelligent
3.	having great knowledge and understanding
4.	important events that celebrate something
5.	to show that you have good feelings for someone or something

C Follow these steps to make predictions about the article below.

1. Think about the title and the subtitle. Write them on the lines.

   _____

   _____

2. Read the three headings. Write them on the lines.

   _____

   _____

   _____

3. Look at the picture, and read the caption. Talk about the picture with a partner.

4. Check the ideas you think will be discussed in the article.

   ❑ **a.** a description of the Korean alphabet

   ❑ **b.** how to make Korean food

   ❑ **c.** alphabets around the world

   ❑ **d.** a holiday for the Korean alphabet

   ❑ **e.** the history of the Korean alphabet

CD 2
TR #2

Hangul Day

A Holiday to Celebrate the Korean Alphabet

An Alphabet with Its Own Holiday

1 The Korean alphabet is called Hangul. It is the only alphabet in the world with its own holiday. The holiday is called Hangul Day. Koreans celebrate Hangul Day every year on October 9th. On Hangul Day, there are **ceremonies** to **honor** the alphabet. People give speeches about the importance of Hangul. Schools all over the country have **contests** to choose the best report about Hangul.

The History of Hangul

2 Hangul Day is important because it honors the history of the alphabet. Many years ago, Koreans wrote with Chinese characters. The thousands of Chinese characters were difficult to learn. Most Koreans could not

read or write. Only rich people could go to school and learn these skills. That changed in 1443, when the ruler of Korea, King Sejong, decided to invent a new Korean alphabet. King Sejong believed that all people should be able to learn how to read and write, and his plan worked.

The Success of Hangul

3 After King Sejong invented Hangul, all Koreans could learn how to read and write easily. They didn't have to learn thousands of Chinese characters. They only had to learn the twenty-four letters of the Hangul alphabet. Each letter in the Hangul alphabet has only one sound, and no letters are silent[1]. This makes Hangul simple to learn. King Sejong said, "A **wise** person can learn Hangul in a few hours. Even a **foolish** person can learn it in ten days!"

4 Today, almost everyone in Korea can read and write because Hangul is so simple. By the time most children enter school, they can already read and write. Because of King

In 1443, King Sejong invented an easy new Korean alphabet called Hangul.

....

Sejong and his alphabet, Korea has one of the highest reading rates in the world. ∎

[1] **silent** – not making any sound

After You Read

Comprehension Check

A Scan the article to match each question with the correct answer.

Question	Answer
_____ 1. What alphabet has its own holiday?	a. so everyone could learn how to read and write
_____ 2. When is Hangul Day celebrated?	b. 1443
_____ 3. Who invented Hangul?	c. twenty-four
_____ 4. When was Hangul invented?	d. King Sejong
_____ 5. Why was Hangul invented?	e. October 9th
_____ 6. How many letters does the Hangul alphabet have?	f. Hangul

B Read these statements. If a statement is true, write *T* on the line. If it is false, write *F.*

_____ 1. Koreans honor their alphabet on New Year's Day.

_____ 2. Each letter in the Hangul alphabet has only one sound.

_____ 3. Many letters in Hangul are silent.

_____ 4. Hangul is a difficult alphabet to learn.

_____ 5. Most people in Korea can read and write.

Vocabulary Practice

A Complete each sentence with the correct word.

ceremonies	contests	foolish
honor	wise	

1. On Hangul Day, there are _____ where Koreans give speeches about their alphabet.

2. Hangul is a holiday to _____ the Korean alphabet.

3. King Sejong was very _____. He understood that all Koreans should be able to read and write.

4. King Sejong believed that even a _____ person could learn Hangul quickly.

5. Schools have _____ to choose the best report about Hangul.

B Ask and answer these questions with a partner.

1. What would you wear to a wedding ceremony?
2. Are there any holidays in your country that honor a famous person?
3. Do you think King Sejong was wise? Why or why not?
4. Have you ever done anything foolish? What did you do?
5. Have you ever won a contest? What kind?

SKILL FOR SUCCESS

Understanding Word Parts: The Suffix *-ish*

The suffix *-ish* is used to form adjectives that describe what a person or thing is like. In this chapter, you learned the word *foolish,* which describes someone who is not intelligent.

C Answer each question with the correct word.

childish   clownish   feverish   selfish

1. How would you describe handwriting that looks like a child wrote it? _____

2. How would you describe someone who looks sick and feels very warm? _____

3. How would you describe people who are only concerned with their own interests? _____

4. How would you describe the behavior of someone who acts like a clown? _____

Talk It Over

Discuss these questions as a class.

1. Why was the invention of Hangul important?
2. In your country, can most children read and write before they enter school?
3. Do you know any interesting facts about your alphabet? Share them with the class.

Read Symbols

Look at these symbols, or signs. They are used in many countries around the world to communicate meanings without using words. Match each symbol with the correct meaning.

Symbol   **Meaning**

_____ 1.   a. no parking

_____ 2.   b. restaurant

_____ 3.   c. no smoking

_____ 4.   🚺   **d.** no cell-phone use

_____ 5.   🚫Ⓟ   **e.** men's restroom

_____ 6.   ☎   **f.** mail

_____ 7.   ✉   **g.** first aid / medical help

_____ 8.   📵   **h.** women's restroom

_____ 9.   🚕   **i.** information

_____ 10.   🍴   **j.** telephone

_____ 11.   ❓   **k.** taxi

_____ 12.   ✚   **l.** wheelchair access

Students Save Their Native Language

The Cherokee people are Native Americans. They were among the first people to live in North America. Today, most Cherokee live in parts of Oklahoma and North Carolina. The Cherokee language is one of many Native American languages that is in danger of disappearing.

Before You Read

A Discuss these questions with a partner.

1. How many languages are spoken in your country?
2. Do any of your family members speak a language that you cannot understand? Would you like to learn that language? Why or why not?
3. What do you know about the Native American people?

B Study these words from the article. Write each word next to the correct definition.

accomplishments   community   fluent
kindergarten   weird

1.	the first year of school, for children age five
2.	all the people living in a place
3.	strange and unusual
4.	able to speak or write a language very well
5.	things that you have done well or with success

C Skimming for the Main Idea

Skim the article one time. Then choose the statement you think describes the main idea.

1. Young students in Oklahoma are learning Cherokee.
2. Cherokee is an old language.
3. November is National American Indian Heritage Month.

STUDENTS SAVE THEIR NATIVE LANGUAGE

Young Students Learn Cherokee

1 **Kindergarten** students at Lost City School near Tulsa, Oklahoma, are learning how to speak Cherokee, a Native American language. They speak Cherokee for most of the day. The students learn colors, numbers, and animal names in Cherokee. Students are called by their Native American names.

Singing Songs in Cherokee

2 The students learn how to sing songs in Cherokee, too. When you walk by the music classroom at Lost City School, you hear unusual sounds. The students are singing a popular song called "Old MacDonald Had a Farm." It is about animals on a farm. But the students are not singing in English. They are singing in Cherokee. They sing, "Old MacDonald had a *wa-ga* and a *ka-wo-nu* on his farm." Those words mean *cow* and *duck* in Cherokee.

Why Learn the Cherokee Language?

3 Cherokee is one of 170 Native American languages in the United States. All of them are in danger of disappearing. Almost everyone who can speak and understand Cherokee well is over the age of forty-five. The children at Lost City School are trying to save their native language. The students' goal is to become **fluent** in Cherokee.

Working and Learning Together

4 At Lost City School, students help each other learn Cherokee. The school has 100 students.

Sequoyah was a Cherokee leader. He invented the written Cherokee language.

Sixty-five of the students are Cherokee. Crystal Braden is thirteen years old. She is one of the Cherokee students. Crystal and several of her classmates made a video to teach younger students the Cherokee words for colors. "If we don't learn Cherokee, our grandchildren won't know it," says Crystal.

5 Younger children are teaching older children, too. Kristian Smith is ten years old. He is learning words from his younger brother, Lane. Lane is in kindergarten. "It's **weird**," says Kristian. "I should be teaching him!"

6 The Cherokee word *ga-du-gi* describes the school's work. It means *working together to help the* **community**. November is National American Indian Heritage Month. At that time, people work together to honor the Native American culture and celebrate its **accomplishments**. But at Lost City School, everyone works together all year long.

After You Read

Comprehension Check

Read these statements. If a statement is true, write *T* on the line. If it is false, write *F*.

_____ 1. All students and teachers at Lost City School know how to speak Cherokee.

_____ 2. Kindergarten students learn the names of colors, numbers, and animals in Cherokee.

_____ 3. There are only a few Native American languages in the United States.

_____ 4. All of the Native American languages are in danger of disappearing.

_____ 5. Almost everyone who can speak and understand Cherokee is over the age of forty-five.

_____ 6. American Indian Heritage Month is celebrated in November.

Vocabulary Practice

A Complete each sentence with the correct word(s).

accomplishment	community	fluent
kindergarten	weird	

1. Students at Lost City School start learning to speak Cherokee in _____.

2. People at Lost City School work together to help the _____.

3. When the students graduate, they will be _____ in Cherokee. It will be a big _____ for them.

4. Kristian thinks it is _____ to be learning Cherokee words from his younger brother.

B Ask and answer these questions with a partner.

1. How old are children when they start kindergarten?
2. Do you have a library in your community?
3. What language(s) are you fluent in?
4. What is your biggest accomplishment this year?
5. What is something weird you have seen on the news recently?

Understanding Word Parts: The Prefix _un-_

The prefix _un-_ is one of the most common prefixes in English. _Un-_ is added to a word to mean _not_ or _the opposite of._ For example, the word _unusual_ from the article means _not usual._

C Add the prefix _un-_ to each word. Then write a sentence using the new word. Use your dictionary to help you. Compare sentences with a partner.

1. ＿＿＿happy

＿＿＿＿＿＿＿＿＿＿＿＿＿＿＿＿＿＿＿＿＿＿＿＿＿＿＿＿＿＿

2. ＿＿＿necessary

＿＿＿＿＿＿＿＿＿＿＿＿＿＿＿＿＿＿＿＿＿＿＿＿＿＿＿＿＿＿

3. ＿＿＿popular

＿＿＿＿＿＿＿＿＿＿＿＿＿＿＿＿＿＿＿＿＿＿＿＿＿＿＿＿＿＿

4. ＿＿＿fair

＿＿＿＿＿＿＿＿＿＿＿＿＿＿＿＿＿＿＿＿＿＿＿＿＿＿＿＿＿＿

5. ＿＿＿safe

＿＿＿＿＿＿＿＿＿＿＿＿＿＿＿＿＿＿＿＿＿＿＿＿＿＿＿＿＿＿

Talk It Over

Discuss these questions as a class.

1. Do you think it is important to save languages that are dying? Why or why not?
2. Are any of the languages in your country in danger of disappearing? What are people doing to save these languages?

Tie It All Together

Discussion   Discuss these questions in a small group.

1. What are some reasons to learn a new language?
2. Why is it sometimes difficult to speak another language?
3. What do you think is the best way to learn a new language?
4. What do you think can be done to save dying languages?

Just for Fun   The word *alphabets* has nine letters. Use these letters to make as many other words as you can. You may not use the same letter twice unless it appears twice in the word *alphabets*. Do not use names or foreign words.

      hat

_____   _____   _____

_____   _____   _____

_____   _____   _____

_____   _____   _____

abc NEWS

Video Activity   **Mastering Mandarin**

This video reports on children in the U.S. who are learning to speak Chinese. In your country, do children learn to speak more than one language?

Language Lessons   **A** Study these words and phrases. Then watch the video.

job market   mandatory   master [verb]

B Read these statements and then watch the video again. Choose the statement that describes the main idea.

1. Only a few people teach Chinese in the United States.
2. Chinese is hard to learn.
3. Today, more American children are learning Chinese.

C Discuss these questions with a partner or in a small group.

Do you think people should be required to learn more than one language? Why or why not?

Reader's Journal   Think about the topics you have read about and discussed in this unit. Choose a topic from the list and write about it for ten to twenty minutes. Pick a topic from the following list, or choose one of your own.

- ways to learn a new language
- why you are studying English
- languages spoken in your country

Vocabulary Self-Test

Complete each sentence with the correct word.

A   ceremony   disappear   fluent
      kindergarten   wise

1. Hamid is very _____. People always ask him for his opinions.

2. Many types of plants and animals _____ every year.

3. More than 200 people came to our wedding _____.

4. Charlotte is five years old. She will start _____ in September.

5. Pia is _____ in six languages.

B   accomplishment   community   expressed
      simple   weird

1. It was a big _____ for Jin to learn to play the violin so well.

2. I had a really _____ dream last night. I dreamed I was a dog.

3. Ben _____ his fears to me about losing his job.

4. Jaivir and his wife have worked hard and done a lot for our _____.

5. It only takes a few minutes to make coffee. It's a quick and _____ process.

C   contest   enormous   equal
      foolish   honor

1. Latif said he can't come with us. He has an _____ amount of work to do by tomorrow.

2. You will each get the same amount of cake. I'm going to cut it into eight _____ pieces.

3. My sister is _____. She didn't study at all for her big test.

4. Alex won the pie-eating _____. He ate nine pies!

5. At a special dinner tonight, the company will _____ Ren Li for her important work.

ANIMAL TALES

We share the world with many types of animals. In this unit, you will read about the ways that animals make us laugh and cry, and about how they bring happiness to our lives.

Points to Ponder

Discuss these questions in a small group.

1. What animals do you think are the best pets? Why?

2. How can animals help people? Give some examples.

3. How can people help animals?

Friends with Four Legs

Before You Read

A Discuss these questions with a partner.

1. Have you ever seen a dog that helps people (for example, a dog that helps people who can't see)? What did you notice about the dog?
2. Do you know any animals that do tricks? What kind of tricks?

B Study these words and phrases from the article. Write each word or phrase next to the correct definition.

commands   disabilities   picks up

trains   turn on

1.	to make something start working
2.	holds and lifts something
3.	orders
4.	teaches
5.	diseases or injuries that make it hard for people to do the things that other people do

C Skim the article one time. Circle the correct answer.

The article mainly discusses _____.

1. a school that trains dogs
2. a pet shop that sells dogs
3. how to teach dogs tricks

FRIENDS WITH FOUR LEGS

1 On May 13th, seven students in Farmingdale, New York, graduated from their school. These students did not study history or math. They did not study English or science. These students have four legs. They are dogs! The dogs are students at a special school called Canine Companions for Independence (CCI). The school **trains** dogs to help people with **disabilities**. Then the school gives the dogs to people who need them. The dogs help their owners do many important things.

2 The dogs start school when they are fifteen months old. Their training program is six months long. It costs $20,000 to train each dog. The dogs learn fifty **commands**. For example, they learn how to **turn on** a light with their nose. They also learn how to open a refrigerator door with their teeth. One of the most important commands the dogs learn is to "snuggle." That means the dogs lie down next to people in a loving way.

3 Lacy Tompkins uses a wheelchair. She has a dog named Ruhl. Ruhl graduated from CCI. Lacy loves to snuggle with Ruhl. "He keeps me company[1] and helps me," says Lacy. "He opens drawers and **picks up** things." Both adults and children like getting help from the dogs. Blair Griesmeyer works at CCI. She says, "For children, the dog is sometimes the first best friend they have ever had."

These dogs go to school to learn how to help people.

[1] **keep someone company** – to stay with someone so he or she is not alone

After You Read

Comprehension Check

A Read these statements. If a statement is true, write *T* on the line. If it is false, write *F*.

_____ 1. Students at CCI study English and science.

_____ 2. Dogs at CCI learn how to help people with disabilities.

_____ 3. It's not possible to teach a dog how to open a refrigerator.

_____ 4. One of the most important commands the dogs learn is to snuggle.

_____ 5. Only adults like having help from dogs.

> **F Y I**
>
> *The three most common kinds of dogs that help people with disabilities are Labrador retrievers, golden retrievers, and German shepherds.*

B Circle the correct answer.

1. How many dogs graduated on May 13th?
   a. four
   b. seven
   c. fifteen

2. How old are the dogs when they start school?
   a. two months
   b. six months
   c. fifteen months

3. How long do the dogs go to school at CCI?
   a. six months
   b. two years
   c. fifteen months

4. How many commands do the dogs learn?
   a. five
   b. fifteen
   c. fifty

5. Who graduated from CCI?
   a. Lacy
   b. Rhul
   c. Blair

Vocabulary Practice

A Complete each sentence with the correct word(s) or phrase(s).

commands   disabilities   picks up

trains   turn on

1. The school _____ dogs to help people with

_____.

2. The dogs learn _____ such as "lie down" and "snuggle."

3. The dogs learn how to _____ a light with their nose.

4. Lacy's dog opens drawers and _____ things from the floor.

B Circle the correct answer.

1. If you <u>train</u> a dog, you _____.
   a. give it something to eat
   b. teach it to do something

2. Which is an example of a <u>disability</u>?
   a. a broken leg
   b. a beautiful voice

3. Which is a <u>command</u>?
   a. "Sit down!"
   b. "Are you hungry?"

4. Which could a dog <u>pick up</u> from the floor?
   a. a bed
   b. a shoe

5. Which do you need to <u>turn on</u> to use?
   a. a cell phone
   b. a book

✓ Learning Phrasal Verbs

C Read the paragraph. Match each underlined phrasal verb with the correct picture.

    The dogs at CCI learn many commands. They learn how to <u>turn on</u>
_{a.}
and <u>turn off</u> a light with their nose. The dogs also learn <u>to pick</u> up things
_{b.}   _{c.}
from the floor and give them to their owners.

    Here are some other commands and their meanings.

Car: Tells the dog to <u>get in</u> a car.
_{d.}

Sit: Tells the dog to <u>sit down</u> and stay until the next command is given.
_{e.}

Down: Tells the dog to <u>lie down</u> and stay.
_{f.}

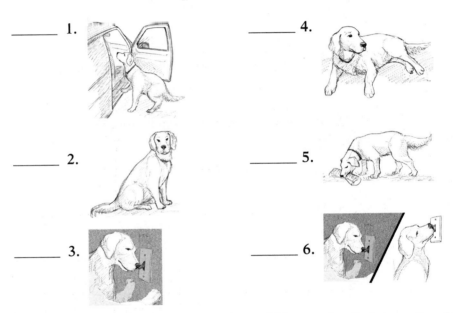

_____ 1.

_____ 2.

_____ 3.

_____ 4.

_____ 5.

_____ 6.

Talk It Over

1. Do you think any other animals could be used to help people with disabilities? Which animals?
2. Do you think robots could help people with disabilities in the same way that dogs can? Why or why not?

A Baby Panda Gets a Name

Before You Read

A Discuss these questions with a partner.

1. Do you like to visit zoos? Does your city have a zoo?
2. What are your favorite animals to see at the zoo?
3. Have you ever seen a giant panda in a zoo?

B Study these words from the article. Write each word next to the correct definition.

diet   habitat   rare

starve   vote

1.	to die or become sick because you do not have enough to eat
2.	the food that you eat
3.	not happening or seen very often
4.	to express your choice, especially by marking a paper or by raising your hand
5.	the place where a plant or animal lives

C You are going to read an article about the birth of a baby panda. Check the statements you think are true about pandas.

❑ 1. There are not many pandas in the world today.

❑ 2. Most pandas live in China.

❑ 3. Pandas eat many different foods.

❑ 4. Most baby pandas are healthy when they are born.

❑ 5. Scientists are trying to help pandas have more babies.

CD2
TR #6

A Baby Panda Gets a Name

A Baby Panda Is Born

1 Mei Xiang is a giant panda from China. She lives at the National Zoo in Washington, D.C. Recently, Mei Xiang had a baby. The baby's father is Tian Tian. People in Washington and around the world were very excited when the baby panda was born. Baby pandas are special and unusual.

Choosing a Name for the Baby

2 The National Zoo decided not to name the panda until he was 100 days old. While they were waiting, some people gave the panda a nickname. They nicknamed him Butterstick because he was the size of a stick of butter.

3 The National Zoo asked people to choose a name for the baby panda. People could **vote** online for their favorite name. About 180,000 people voted. These were the possible names:

1. Hua Sheng (*China-Washington, or Magnificent*)
2. Sheng Hua (*Washington-China, or Magnificent*)

3. Tai Shan (*Peaceful Mountain*)
4. Long Shan (*Dragon Mountain*)
5. Qiang Qiang (*Strong* or *Powerful*)

The zoo announced the winning name during a naming ceremony on October 17th. The winning name was Tai Shan.

Giant Pandas Face Giant Problems

4 Giant pandas are very **rare.** They are endangered animals. That's why scientists and animal lovers were so happy about the birth of a baby panda. There are several reasons why pandas are endangered. One reason is that giant pandas do not have babies very often. And many baby pandas are not healthy. Six out of ten giant panda babies die soon after birth.

5 Giant pandas are also endangered because of their **diet** and **habitat**. Giant pandas have a very special diet. The only food they eat is bamboo. Pandas have to eat about 40 pounds (18 kg) of this plant a day to live. But there are not many bamboo forests[1] left in the world. When there is not enough bamboo for the pandas to eat, they **starve** to death. China

Text 6

is the only place where pandas can still live in bamboo forests. There are only about 1,000 pandas living in China's bamboo forests.

Pandas love to eat bamboo.

....

There are 120 more pandas living in zoos around the world.

Saving the Pandas

6 China and the United States are working together to save the pandas. They are helping giant pandas like Mei Xiang have more babies. China sent Mei Xiang and Tian Tian to the United States so scientists there could study the pandas. When he is three years old, Tai Shen will go to China to live. After living in the United States for ten years, his parents will return home, too.

[1] **forests** – areas with a lot of trees and plants

After You Read

Comprehension Check

A Check the topics discussed in the article.

❏ 1. the many plants and animals of China

❏ 2. how to care for a baby panda

❏ 3. how the baby panda was named

❏ 4. problems for pandas

❏ 5. zoos around the world

❏ 6. how scientists are helping pandas

B Circle the correct answer.

1. Where does Mei Xiang live?

a. in a zoo in the United States

b. in a zoo in China

c. in a forest in China

2. Why did people nickname the baby panda Butterstick?

a. because he smelled like butter

b. because he liked to eat butter

c. because he was the size of a stick of butter

3. What was the baby panda named?

a. Tai Shan

b. Hua Sheng

c. Long Shan

4. What do pandas eat?

a. forests

b. butter

c. bamboo

5. What are scientists in China and the United States trying to do?

a. vote for names

b. save the pandas

c. open more zoos

6. When will the baby panda move to China?

a. when he is 100 days old

b. when he is three years old

c. in ten years

 SKILL FOR SUCCESS

Understanding Cause and Effect

When you read, it is important to understand the **causes** (reasons) and **effects** (results) of a situation. In "Giant Pandas Face Giant Problems," the author describes the reasons pandas are endangered.

C Go back to the article. Find three reasons (causes) that giant pandas are endangered (effect). Write the causes in the boxes.

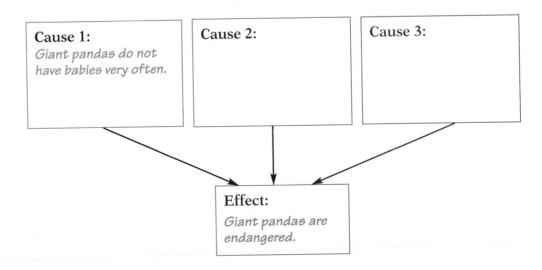

Cause 1:
Giant pandas do not have babies very often.

Cause 2:

Cause 3:

Effect:
Giant pandas are endangered.

F Y I

In China, the panda is a symbol of peace.

A Complete each sentence with the correct word.

diet   habitat   rare   starve   vote

1. Giant pandas have a special _____. They eat only bamboo.

2. If pandas do not have enough to eat, they will _____.

3. Many people went online to _____ for the baby panda's name.

4. There are not many pandas left in the world. They are _____ animals.

5. Pandas live in the bamboo forests of China. These forests are the panda's _____.

B Ask and answer these questions with a partner.

1. In your country, how old do you have to be in order to <u>vote</u>?
2. What is unusual about the giant panda's <u>diet</u>?
3. What other <u>rare</u> animals do you know about? Where are their <u>habitats</u>?
4. If you eat a <u>lot</u>, will you <u>starve</u>?

✓ **Learning Synonyms and Antonyms**

C Decide if the following pairs of words are synonyms or antonyms. If they are synonyms, circle *S*. If they are antonyms, circle *A*.

1. vote   choose   S   A

2. starve   be hungry   S   A

3. healthy   well   S   A

4. excited   sad   S   A

5. rare   common   S   A

Valley Zoo

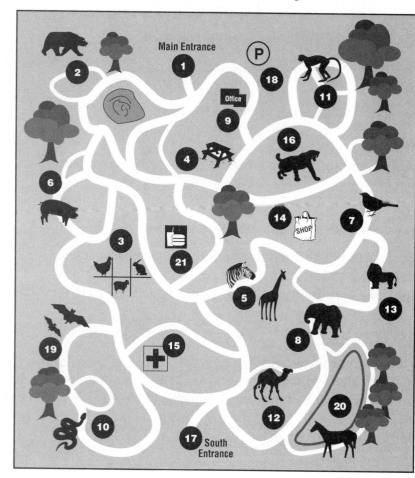

1. Main Entrance
2. Bear Area
3. Please Pet Me (Children's Zoo)
4. Picnic Place
5. African Plains (Zebras, Giraffes)
6. Small Mammal House
7. Bird Cage
8. Elephant Area
9. Business Office
10. Snake Center
11. Monkey Island
12. Camel Rides
13. Lion's Den
14. Zoo Shop
15. First Aid
16. Tiger Exhibit
17. South Entrance
18. Parking
19. Bat Cave
20. Pony Rides
21. Zoo Cafe

Where would you go to . . .

1. have a picnic lunch with your friends? _____

2. take a child on a camel ride? _____

3. watch the monkeys? _____

4. buy your friend a gift from the zoo? _____

5. look at the birds? _____

A Lost Cat Comes Home

Before You Read

A Discuss these questions with a partner.

1. Do you or does anyone you know have a pet cat?
2. Do you think cats are good pets? Why or why not?
3. Did you ever have a pet that got lost? What happened?

B Study these words from the article. Write each word next to the correct definition.

curious   exhausted   glad   journey   thin

1.	happy
2.	very tired
3.	wanting to learn or try new things
4.	not fat
5.	a long trip

✓ **Predicting**

C Follow these steps to make predictions about the article on page 124.

1. Think about the title.
2. Read the three headings.
3. Look at the picture, and read the caption.
4. Make a prediction. What do you think the article will be about?

_____

A Lost Cat Comes Home

1 Emily is a gray and white cat. She is a **curious** cat. Recently, she took a 4,000-mile trip. But Emily didn't plan to take a trip. And she certainly didn't plan to take such a long **journey**.

A Curious Cat

2 Emily lives with the McElhiney family in Wisconsin. One day in September, Emily took a walk. She walked into the warehouse[1] of a paper company near her house. Inside the building, Emily crawled into a box of paper. The box traveled by truck to Chicago. From Chicago, it went by ship across the Atlantic Ocean! Emily was inside the box all the way.

3 Emily ended up at another company—in France! On October 24th, one of the workers at the company found Emily. It was the cat's first birthday. She was **thin** and thirsty, but she was still healthy.

4 Workers at the factory looked at the tags around Emily's neck. The tags had the phone number of the cat's veterinarian[2] in Wisconsin. The workers called the veterinarian. Then the veterinarian called the McElhineys. He told them that Emily was safe.

Emily the cat flies home first class after a long trip.

Emily Flies Home First Class

5 Continental Airlines gave Emily a free plane ticket home to the United States. She flew home first class, in the best part of the airplane. She sat in a $6,000 seat! On the flight home, Emily was served a nice dinner of salmon. But she didn't want the fish. She wanted French cat food.

---

[1] **warehouse** – a large building for holding items before they are sold

[2] **veterinarian** – a doctor who takes care of animals

A Happy Homecoming

6 Emily arrived in Newark, New Jersey. From there, she flew to Wisconsin. Gaylia McLeod works for Continental Airlines. She flew with Emily. Emily's family met the cat at the airport. They were very **glad** to see her. There were also lots of news reporters and photographers at the happy event.

7 Has Emily changed since her adventure? Does her meow[3] have a French accent now? Her owner, Lesley McElhiney, said Emily was a little quieter and wiser when she got home. She was thin and **exhausted**, but she is still a curious cat!

[3] **meow** – the sound that a cat makes

After You Read

Comprehension Check

A Read these statements. If a statement is true, write *T* on the line. If it is false, write *F*.

_____ 1. Emily lives with a family in France.

_____ 2. Emily's family sent her on a long trip.

_____ 3. Emily crossed the Atlantic Ocean by ship.

_____ 4. When a worker found Emily, she was very sick.

_____ 5. Emily flew home first class.

B Circle the correct answer.

1. Where is Emily from?
   a. Chicago
   b. Wisconsin
   c. France

2. How did Emily get from Wisconsin to Chicago?
   a. by truck
   b. by ship
   c. by plane

3. When was Emily found?

    a. on October 24th

    b. in September

    c. at the airport

4. Who flew home with Emily?

    a. Gaylia McLeod

    b. a factory worker

    c. Lesley McElhiney

Vocabulary Practice

A Complete each sentence with the correct word.

curious	exhausted	glad
journey	thin	

1. Emily is a _____ cat. She likes to do new things.

2. Emily went on a _____ to France.

3. After her trip, Emily was very _____. She needed to eat more.

4. Emily was also _____. She needed to sleep.

5. The McElhineys were _____ to see Emily again.

B Answer these questions. Check *Yes* or *No*.

	Yes	No
1. If you are <u>glad</u> about something, are you sad?		
2. If you want to be <u>thin</u>, do you eat a lot of sweet foods?		
3. If you go on a long <u>journey</u>, do you leave home?		
4. When you are <u>exhausted</u>, do you want to sleep?		
5. If you don't want to know anything about your friend's new car, are you <u>curious</u> about it?		

SKILL FOR SUCCESS

Understanding Pronouns

Pronouns replace nouns. They are small words, but they are very important. Study these subject pronouns.

Singular	Plural
I	*we*
you	*you*
he, she, it	*they*

C Read these sentences. Write the noun that each underlined pronoun replaces.

1. One day in September, Emily took a walk. <u>She</u> walked into a warehouse near her house.
   She = <u>Emily</u>

2. The box traveled by truck to Chicago. From Chicago, <u>it</u> went by ship across the Atlantic Ocean!
   it = _____

3. Then the veterinarian called the McElhineys. <u>He</u> told them that Emily was safe.
   He = _____

4. Emily's family met the cat at the airport. <u>They</u> were very glad to see her.
   They = _____

Talk It Over

Discuss these questions as a class.

1. What do you think are the most curious animals?
2. A popular English saying is "Curiosity killed the cat." What do you think this means?
3. Do you think it is good to be curious? Can curiosity ever be unsafe?

Skim each short news article to find the main idea. Then write the best headline above each article.

Headlines

A New Bug Zoo
Hua Mei Is Her Name
Hundreds of Pets Get New Homes
The Last Great Race

---

1. _____ *Hua Mei Is Her Name* _____

There was a big party on December 1st at the San Diego Zoo in California. It was a birthday party for a giant panda cub who was 100 days old. The cub was born at the zoo on August 21st. The party was a traditional Chinese ceremony. Many people came to the party. Chinese officials decided to name the panda cub Hua Mei, which means *China-U.S.A.* The name also means *magnificent.* Hua Mei is both!

---

2. _____

There was a lot of noise in a Greenfield parking lot on Saturday. It came from the hundreds of animals that were waiting there. Everywhere you looked, there were dogs, cats, puppies, and kittens. The animals were waiting to be adopted by residents of Greenfield. A club called No More Homeless Pets brought the animals to the parking lot. It was a successful day for the animals and their new owners. More than 250 animals found new homes!

3. _____

A new zoo opened in town this week. But it isn't a regular zoo. It's a bug zoo! The zoo has lots of live bugs and spiders. There are tarantulas, bees, colorful butterflies, beetles, huge grasshoppers, and more. The friendly zoo guides will let you hold some of the bugs. The Bug Zoo also has a gift shop. It sells insect-related products. For example, there are insect snacks you can eat, insect toys, books about insects, and T-shirts. Come enjoy a day at the Bug Zoo.

4. _____

The Iditarod Sled Dog Race began on Sunday in Anchorage, Alaska, and ends in Nome, Alaska. The race is exciting. It is also important because of its history. In 1925, many people in Nome got very sick. The medicine they needed was 1,000 miles away in Anchorage. Twenty dog-sled teams went to Anchorage to get the medicine. They got it in five days and saved many lives. Today, the Iditarod honors them. It is often called "The Last Great Race." The first team arrives in Nome in about ten days. More teams arrive every day for a week. The race is very difficult. It is very cold, and there can be blizzards. The mountain trails are dangerous. The Iditarod really is the "Last Great Race."

Take a Survey

Interview five of your classmates. Ask them to answer the questions in the chart. Share your survey results with your classmates.

Classmate's Name	What animal do you think is the best pet?	What is your favorite animal to watch at a zoo?	What animal would you like to be?

Discussion

Discuss these questions in a small group.

1. Do you think animals are happy in zoos? Why or why not?
2. Do you know someone who owns an unusual pet? What is it?
3. How can people help save endangered animals?

Just for Fun

Find and circle these words from the unit. The words may be horizontal (→) or vertical (↓). One word has been found for you.

ANIMALS
BABIES
BEES
CAT
COMMANDS
DOG
FLIGHT
GIANT
GRADUATE
PANDA
PET
REPORTERS
SALMON
VETERINARIAN
ZOO

```
X  L  F  M  A  N  I  M  A  L  S  W  L  V  C  F
V  R  F  S  E  U  Y  C  K  A  S  Q  P  K  P  L
B  E  K  Y  P  X  P  L  Z  M  G  C  G  R  A  I
V  P  D  U  E  Q  J  C  J  Z  I  A  X  W  N  G
E  O  I  B  A  B  I  E  S  P  A  T  O  Q  D  H
T  R  C  E  P  Q  A  C  Z  B  N  C  W  R  A  T
E  T  D  Q  K  H  B  S  R  A  T  L  N  Y  Q  R
R  E  J  O  E  G  R  A  D  U  A  T  E  B  M  U
I  R  H  R  J  H  F  R  H  F  A  S  A  C  E  W
N  S  C  O  M  M  A  N  D  S  G  A  D  A  T  O
A  S  I  Z  H  A  F  H  Z  I  M  L  F  M  N  D
R  Q  G  O  E  M  G  Q  M  L  V  M  B  E  E  S
I  T  D  O  Y  H  Y  Z  F  H  P  O  C  P  U  D
A  Y  V  F  J  Q  R  F  E  I  N  N  X  E  J  O
N  A  U  H  X  K  R  S  O  W  L  O  C  T  O  G
S  X  V  C  D  W  L  Z  I  R  Y  V  Z  L  Y  J
```

Parrots as Pets

In this video you will learn about pet parrots and their owners. Have you ever seen a parrot? What do you think you will learn about these animals?

A Study these words and phrases. Then watch the video.

captivity   emotional   intelligent

B Read these statements and then watch the video again. If a statement is true, write *T* on the line. If it is false, write *F*.

_____ 1. Many people think parrots are beautiful and intelligent.

_____ 2. Alex can count and identify colors.

_____ 3. Alex speaks Spanish.

_____ 4. Parrots communicate more with words than with actions.

_____ 5. Some people think parrots make difficult pets.

C Discuss these questions with a partner or in a small group.

1. Would you enjoy having a pet parrot? Why or why not?
2. Do you think people should keep parrots as pets? Why or why not? What other animals may not make good pets?

Reader's Journal Think about the topics and ideas you have read about and discussed in this unit. Choose a topic from the list and write about it for ten to twenty minutes. Pick a topic from the following list, or choose one of your own.

- the good and bad things about owning a pet
- how to teach your pet tricks
- an experience you have had with a pet or other animal

Vocabulary Self-Test

Complete each sentence with the correct word or phrase.

A command diet journey
   starve vote

1. I am going to _____ for Juan to be president of our class.

2. Jonathan does not eat good food. His _____ is mostly potato chips, candy, and soda.

3. When you tell a dog to sit, you are giving it a _____.

4. If you don't eat, you'll _____ to death.

5. We went on a three-week bus trip around Europe. It was quite a

   _____.

B exhausted glad pick up
   rare trains

1. Daniela was _____ after she ran the race. She went home to take a nap.

2. I am so _____ you like the sweater I gave you.

3. Christina _____ the workers at the museum to help visitors.

4. Snowstorms are _____ in warm places.

5. Please _____ the pencil. It fell on the floor.

C curious disability habitat
   thin turn on

1. Joanne lost her hearing when she was ten years old. She has learned to

   live with her _____.

2. Please _____ the light. It's so dark, I can't see in here.

3. If you want to know about something, you are _____.

4. The opposite of *fat* is _____.

5. Pandas live in bamboo forests. That is their _____.

SPORTS STORIES

Playing sports is important to many people. You can learn a lot by playing and practicing a sport. You can also learn a lot by reading about sports. In this unit, you'll learn some interesting things about sports and the people who enjoy them.

Points to Ponder

Discuss these questions in a small group.

1. What is the woman in the first photo doing? What sport are the men in the second photo playing?

2. Do you have a favorite sport? What is it?

3. What sports are popular in your country?

A Marathon Marriage

Before You Read

A Discuss these questions with a partner

1. Do you like to run? Have you ever been in a race?
2. A marathon is a 26.2-mile (42.258-kilometer) race. Have you ever run in a marathon? Would you like to run in a marathon?
3. Describe a traditional wedding in your country. What does the bride usually wear? What does the groom usually wear?

B Study these words from the article. Write each word or phrase next to the correct definition.

attended   couple   exchanged

invite   took place

1.	two people who are married or have a romantic relationship
2.	happened
3.	went to an event
4.	gave something to someone and received something from him or her
5.	to ask someone to come to an event

C You are going to read about a man and woman who got married while they were running in a marathon. What are three things you hope to learn from the article?

1. _____

2. _____

3. _____

A MARATHON MARRIAGE

1   Ken Ashby and Linda Kelley are both runners. They have run lots of marathons. On Sunday, they ran the White Rock Marathon in Dallas, Texas. But this marathon was more than just a race for the **couple**. In fact, it was a very special marathon for them. Ken and Linda got married during the race! The ten-minute wedding ceremony **took place** just past Mile 19. The bride and groom were wearing running clothes and sneakers.

2   Ken and Linda decided just a few days before the marathon to get married. They didn't send out formal wedding invitations. They e-mailed their friends to **invite** them to the wedding.

3   Ken ran the first part of the marathon alone. He wore a sign on his back that said, "Getting married at 19." When he stopped at Mile 19, Linda was there waiting for him. She was wearing a white veil with her running clothes and sneakers. The best man[1], Scott McKissick, and the maid of honor[2], Frances McKissick, are also runners. They ran in the marathon, too. About forty of Ken and Linda's friends, mostly runners, **attended** the ceremony. Tim Epting is a runner and a minister[3]. He performed the wedding ceremony. During the ceremony, the couple **exchanged** rings and kissed. Tim said a prayer and gave a short talk. He compared marriages to marathons. Later, Ken told reporters he hopes marriage is easier than marathons!

4   After the ceremony, Ken changed the sign on his back to "Got married at 19." Then he and his new bride ran the last 7.2 miles (11.6 kilometers) of the marathon together. At the end of the race, Ken carried his new wife across the finish line. It was a great day for a marathon and for a wedding.

[1] **best man** – a male friend who helps a man at his wedding

[2] **maid of honor** – a female friend who helps a woman at her wedding

[3] **minister** – a religious leader

After You Read

Comprehension Check

A Read these statements. If a statement is true, write *T* on the line. If it is false, write *F*.

_____ 1. Ken and Linda run in marathons.

_____ 2. Ken and Linda got married in a church in Dallas, Texas.

_____ 3. The wedding ceremony took about an hour.

_____ 4. Linda ran the whole White Rock Marathon.

_____ 5. Frances McKissick was the maid of honor.

_____ 6. Ken carried Linda across the finish line.

_____ 7. Tim Epting performed the wedding ceremony.

SKILL FOR SUCCESS ✔

Recognizing Time Order

Most stories are written in **time order**. That means the writer tells you what happened first, second, third, and so on. As you read, look for clues that give you information about the order of events. Dates, times, and other words can help you. Here are some common words that show time order.

when	*before*	*first*	*next*	*last*
then	*after*	*second*	*later*	*finally*

B Number these events so they are in the correct time order.

_____ Tim Epting performed the wedding ceremony.

__1__ Ken and Linda decided to get married.

_____ Ken changed the sign on his back to "Got married at 19."

_____ The bride and groom ran the last 7.2 miles of the marathon together.

_____ They e-mailed their friends to invite them to the wedding.

_____ Ken carried Linda across the finish line.

_____ Ken ran the first part of the marathon wearing a sign that said "Getting married at 19."

Vocabulary Practice

A Complete each sentence with the correct word or phrase.

attended   couple   exchanged
invite   took place

1. The White Rock Marathon was a special race for Ken and Linda. The _____ got married during the race.

2. Linda and Ken e-mailed their friends to _____ them to the wedding.

3. Forty of their friends _____ the wedding.

4. Ken and Linda _____ rings during the ceremony.

5. The wedding _____ at Mile 19.

B Circle the correct answer.

1. There are _____ people in a <u>couple</u>.
   a. two
   b. three

2. If you <u>exchange</u> rings with someone, you _____ .
   a. keep your own ring
   b. give the other person your ring

3. If you <u>attend</u> a party, you _____ .
   a. plan the party
   b. go to the party

4. If you <u>invite</u> people to your wedding, you _____ .
   a. want them to come
   b. don't want them to come

5. If your wedding <u>took place</u> in a hotel, you _____ .
   a. got married there
   b. went there after the wedding

✓ **Learning Expressions with *Take***

C Match each expression with the correct definition. Work in a small group.

Expression	Definition
_____ 1. take over	**a.** to remove something from a place or container
_____ 2. take out	**b.** to look or act like an older member of your family
_____ 3. take after	**c.** to move from the ground and begin to fly
_____ 4. take back	**d.** to control or do something that someone else was doing before
_____ 5. take off	**e.** to return something

D Complete each sentence with the correct expression from Exercise C.

1. The dentist had to _____ two of my teeth.

2. Please _____ the library books today.

3. The plane is going to _____ in an hour.

4. All the children have brown hair and green eyes. They _____ their mother.

5. When Stan leaves the company, Paul will _____ his job.

Talk It Over

Discuss these questions as a class.

1. Are you married? If you are, did you have an unusual wedding or a traditional one?
2. How do you feel about unusual weddings, such as getting married during a marathon?
3. What other unusual weddings have you heard of or read about?
4. What did Ken mean when he said that he hopes marriage is easier than a marathon?

Who Is Tiger Woods?

Before You Read

A Discuss these questions with a partner.

1. Is golf popular in your country?
2. Do you play golf? Why or why not?
3. Do you like to watch golf?
4. Look at the photograph. Do you recognize this man? What do you know about him?

B Study these words from the article. Write each word next to the correct definition.

athletes   multicultural   professional
proud   substitute

1.	having many cultural backgrounds
2.	people who are good at sports
3.	feeling happy about something good that you do or have
4.	doing an activity for money
5.	something that you can exchange for another thing

Who Is Tiger Woods?

1   Tiger Woods is one of the most famous golfers in the world. In fact, he's one of the most famous **athletes** alive today. He was born on December 30, 1975, in Long Beach, California. His real name is Eldrick Woods. How did he get the name Tiger? His father, Earl Woods, gave him the nickname when he was a young boy. Why Tiger? Earl chose the name to honor his South Vietnamese friend Nguyen Phong. Nguyen Phong saved Earl's life in the Vietnam War. His nickname was Tiger, too.

2   Tiger Woods is truly a **multicultural** person. His mother, Kultida, is Asian. She is from Thailand. She is part Thai, part Chinese, and part Dutch. Tiger's father was multicultural, too. He was part African American, or black, and part American Indian. What is Tiger? Tiger describes himself as a Cablinasian. *Ca* is for *Caucasian. Bl* is for *black. In* is for *Indian. Asian* is for *Asian.* Tiger is very **proud** of his multicultural background.

3   Tiger has always loved golf. When he was only six months old, he liked to watch as his father hit golf balls. Tiger showed his golf skills on television when he was just two years old. There was a story about Tiger in *Golf Digest* magazine when he was five. By age fifteen, Tiger had won several important amateur tournaments[1]. Tiger Woods became a **professional** golfer in 1996. That year, *Sports Illustrated* magazine named him Sportsman of the Year. In 1997, he played in and won the Masters Tournament, one of the most important professional golf competitions. Tiger was the youngest person ever to win this tournament. He won the Masters again in 2001, 2002, and 2005. In 2006, Tiger won the British open for the second year in a row. It was his first big win after his father's death earlier that year. The victory was very special and emotional for Tiger.

TIGER'S WINS IN MAJORS
The Masters
1997, 2001, 2002, 2005
The U.S. Open
2000, 2002
The British Open
2000, 2005, 2006
The PGA Championship
1999, 2000, 2006

4   Tiger works very hard. He practices many hours every day. A newspaper reporter asked Tiger how he became such a good golfer. He answered, "There is no **substitute** for hard work." Tiger's hard work has brought him a lot of success and money. Nike gave Tiger $40 million to help sell Nike products. Soon many other companies hired him to help sell their products, too.

5   Tiger also wants to be a good influence[2] on people, especially young people. He says being a good example for other people is more important than playing golf. In 1996, Tiger and his father started the Tiger Woods Foundation. It raises millions of dollars to help young people reach their goals.

[1] **amateur tournaments** – sports contests that you do not get money to play in

[2] **influence** – someone or something that affects others

After You Read

Comprehension Check

A Check the topics discussed in the article.

❏ 1. when Tiger became interested in golf
❏ 2. how Tiger got his nickname
❏ 3. what other sports Tiger likes
❏ 4. how Tiger describes himself
❏ 5. which tournaments Tiger has won
❏ 6. what Tiger likes to eat

B Circle the correct answer.

1. Why did Earl Woods nickname his son Tiger?

   a. because his son was very strong

   b. because he did not like the name Eldrick

   c. to honor his friend

2. Where is Tiger's mother from?

   a. Vietnam

   b. Thailand

   c. the United States

3. How old was Tiger when *Golf Digest* wrote a story about him?

   a. six months old

   b. two years old

   c. five years old

4. When did Tiger become a professional golfer?

   a. in 1996

   b. in 1997

   c. in 2000

5. What does the Tiger Woods Foundation do?

   a. publishes *Sports Illustrated*

   b. sells golf products

   c. helps young people reach their goals

6. Which of the following is a magazine?

   a. The Masters Tournament

   b. *Golf Digest*

   c. The Tiger Woods Foundation

Two sports invented in the United States are basketball (invented in 1891) and baseball (invented in 1839).

✓ **Scanning for Information**

C Scan the chart in the article to answer each question. Work as fast as you can.

1. In what years did Tiger win the British Open? _____

2. What two tournaments did Tiger win in 2005? _____

   _____

3. How many times has Tiger won the U.S. Open? _____

4. When was Tiger's first majors win? _____

Vocabulary Practice

A Complete each sentence with the correct word(s).

athletes   multicultural   professional

proud   substitute

1. Tiger is very _____ of his _____ background.

2. Tiger is one of the most famous _____ in the world.

3. Tiger practices golf for hours. He says there is no _____ for hard work.

4. In 1996, Tiger Woods became a _____ golfer. He earns a lot of money playing the sport.

B Circle the correct answer.

1. A <u>professional</u> tennis player _____.
   a. gets money to play tennis
   b. only plays for fun

2. If someone is a good <u>athlete</u>, he or she is _____.
   a. not interested in sports
   b. very good at playing sports

3. A restaurant that serves <u>multicultural</u> food serves _____.
   a. food from many countries
   b. only French food

4. Which is a <u>substitute</u> for a pencil? _____.
   a. a pen
   b. paper

5. If you are <u>proud</u> of your work, you _____.
   a. feel good about it
   b. are disappointed by it

F Y I

In Canada, ice hockey is the most popular sport. In the Netherlands, the most popular sport is ice skating. In Thailand, it's kite flying.

Understanding Word Parts: The Prefix *multi-*

The prefix *multi-* is added to a word to mean *many*. For example, the word *multicultural* from the article means *having many cultural backgrounds*.

C Add the prefix *multi-* to each word. Then write the definition of the new word. Use your dictionary to help you.

1. _____millionaire

_____

2. _____purpose

_____

3. _____national

_____

4. _____talented

_____

5. _____colored

_____

D Complete each sentence with the correct word from Exercise C. Compare answers with a partner.

1. Jason can play the piano, draw pictures, and play baseball very well.

   He is _____.

2. Pamela is very rich. She is a _____.

3. She is wearing a red, blue, purple, and yellow dress. It's a

   _____ dress.

4. The company has offices in many countries. It's a _____
   company.

5. We use this room for many different activities. We study, play games,

   watch TV, and listen to music here. It's a _____ room.

Talk It Over

Discuss these questions as a class.

1. Do you think Tiger Woods is a good example for children? Why or why not?
2. If you could meet Tiger Woods, what questions would you ask him?
3. If you could meet any famous athlete, who would you want to meet? What questions would you ask him or her?

Read a Sports Section

Scan the TV schedule from the sports section of a newspaper to answer these questions.

1. When can you watch the Boston Red Sox play against the New York Yankees? _____

2. What channel is showing golf in the afternoon? _____

3. Where will the tennis championship be played? _____

4. When can you watch a soccer game on TV? _____

Saturday Sports on TV

SPORT	PROGRAM/EVENT	TIME	CHANNEL
Baseball	This Week in Baseball	12:30 P.M.	25
	Boston Red Sox *vs.* New York Yankees	7:00 P.M.	7
Golf	Scotland National Championship	10:00 A.M.	5
	Players Championship, Dearborn, Michigan	2:00 P.M.	4
Soccer	Tampa Bay at Chicago	2:30 P.M.	7
Tennis	Hall of Fame Championship, Newport, Rhode Island	2:00 P.M.	12 and 25

UNIT 7

CHAPTER 3

The "Ultimate" Game

Before You Read

A Discuss these questions with a partner.

1. What do you think it means for someone to be a "good sport"?
2. The word *ultimate* describes something that is the best or the most important. Do you know about the sport called Ultimate?

B Study these words from the article. Write each word next to the correct definition.

competitive   object   rules
score   trust

1.	things that tell you what you can and cannot do
2.	wanting to win or be the best
3.	to win a point in a game
4.	purpose
5.	to believe someone is honest or good

The "Ultimate" Game

1   Ultimate is a very popular team sport. A group of high school students in Maplewood, New Jersey, invented the game of Ultimate in the early 1960s. Ultimate grew in popularity in the 1970s, and today it is the fastest-growing team sport in the world. Ultimate is played by thousands of people in more than fifty countries all over the world.

2   Ultimate is played with a plastic disc that players throw to each other. Ultimate combines the skills used in soccer and basketball. Ultimate players must be fast like soccer players. They must be able to jump like basketball players and pass the disc like basketball players pass a ball. Ultimate is a very fast game, so it is exciting to watch and to play.

3   During an Ultimate game, each team has seven players on the field. The **object** of the game is to **score** points. When a player catches the disc in the end zone, his or her team earns a point. The first team to score fifteen points wins the game.

End Zone   End Zone
                                        40 yds
                                        (37m)

25 yds   70 yds   25 yds
(23m)   (64m)   (23m)

4   The **rules** of Ultimate are easy to learn. Players cannot run while they are holding the disc. They must throw the disc to one of their teammates to move it down the field. They must not let the disc touch the ground. Finally, players are not allowed to touch each other.

5   In Ultimate, it is important to play in a fair and honest way. This means having good sportsmanship. There are no referees[1] in Ultimate. The players on the field decide when someone isn't following the rules. There are usually no coaches, either. Ultimate players **trust** one another to be honest, fair, hardworking, and **competitive**. This combination of trust and competition makes Ultimate the ultimate sport to many people.

[1] **referees** – people who make sure that players follow the rules of a game

After You Read

Comprehension Check

A   Write the paragraph number that answers each question.

1. Which paragraph talks about sportsmanship? _____

2. Which paragraph explains how players earn points in an Ultimate game? _____

3. Which paragraph talks about the skills an Ultimate player must have? _____

4. Which paragraph tells when Ultimate was invented? _____

B   Read these statements. If a statement is true, write *T* on the line. If it is false, write *F*.

_____ 1. Ultimate is played only in New Jersey.

_____ 2. There are ten players on an Ultimate team.

_____ 3. The first team to get fifteen points wins.

_____ 4. A player must not run with the disc.

_____ 5. A referee makes sure Ultimate players follow the rules.

Vocabulary Practice

A Complete each sentence with the correct word(s).

competitive   object   rules
score   trust

1. The _____ of Ultimate is to _____ points.

2. Ultimate players are _____. They all want to win.

3. The _____ of Ultimate are easy to learn.

4. Ultimate players _____ one another to be honest and fair.

B Circle the correct answer.

1. The <u>rules</u> of a game tell you _____.

   a. the history of the game

   b. what you can and can't do in the game

2. The <u>object</u> of most games is to _____.

   a. win

   b. lose

3. If you <u>trust</u> a friend, you _____.

   a. think he is an honest person

   b. think he is a fun person

4. When you <u>score</u> a point, you _____.

   a. are happy because you won the point

   b. are sad because you lost the point

5. A <u>competitive</u> person _____.

   a. likes to win

   b. doesn't care about winning

C Ask and answer these questions with a partner.

1. Who is the most <u>competitive</u> person you know?

2. Do you think it is important for players on the same team to <u>trust</u> one another?

3. How do you <u>score</u> points in soccer?

4. Do you like games with difficult <u>rules</u>?

5. What is the <u>object</u> of a race?

Understanding Word Forms

Some words have the same **form** but are used as different parts of speech with different meanings. For example:

*The game has ten **rules**.* (In this sentence, *rules* is used as a noun.)
*The king **rules** the country.* (In this sentence, *rules* is used as a verb.)

D Read the sentences and decide if the underlined word is a noun or a verb. Check the correct box. Use your dictionary to help you.

	Noun	Verb
1. It's important to follow the rules.		
2. He rules the company and has a lot of power.		
3. I trust my parents to make good decisions.		
4. Trust is an important part of friendship.		
5. What is the object of the game?		
6. Do you object to starting the meeting now?		
7. The final score was 5 to 3.		
8. It is difficult to score many points in a soccer game.		

Improve Your Reading Speed

Look at the first word in each row. Circle the words that are the same as the first word. Work as fast as you can.

1. **fast**	last	fake	faster	fail	fame	faster	fast
2. **are**	all	rare	are	are	art	ant	are
3. **ages**	again	rages	rage	age	ages	again	agent
4. **team**	team	teach	take	lean	team	teach	tell
5. **best**	rest	nest	bean	dear	best	better	bead
6. **rare**	rate	rain	race	rake	rare	rage	rare
7. **tail**	take	tame	tale	tail	tan	fail	tail
8. **head**	height	heart	head	hide	hair	heir	hear
9. **buck**	bulk	bull	buck	bugle	bulb	build	buck
10. **pack**	pack	pink	perk	poke	part	pack	pick

Scan each short news article to find the main idea. Then write the best headline above the article.

Headlines

Students Learn Karate-do
Championship Goes to Brown
London to Host Summer Olympics
Teen Golfer Goes Professional

1. _____

Brown University has the country's best Ultimate team this year. This morning, Brown beat Carleton College. It was the final game to win the National Championship. The score was 15 to 10. It was an exciting game. Both teams played well. When Brown scored the winning point, players and fans ran onto the field. One player said, "Winning feels great! We had a dream. We all worked really hard to achieve it. Now, we are the champs. Nobody can take that away from us."

2. _____

Londoners were very happy today. It was announced that the 2012 Summer Olympic Games will take place in London, England, for the first time in more than fifty years. Thousands of people cheered and waved flags in Trafalgar Square in London. They watched the announcement on huge television screens in the square. British prime minister Tony Blair said it was "a momentous day for London." London also hosted the Olympic Games in 1908 and 1948. It is the only city in the world to host the Olympics three times.

3. _____

Tomorrow, students in Lawrence can learn Karate-do from one of the world's best teachers. His name is William Millerson, and he is a black belt in Karate-do. He will give free Karate classes at Lawrence High School at 10 a.m. and 1 p.m. Karate-do is very popular in Japan, England, China, and Canada. There are only 100 Karate-do schools in the United States. Students who take classes will learn about the history of Karate-do. They will also learn several Karate moves. More than 300 people plan

to come. If you do, please wear comfortable, loose clothing.

4. _____

Michelle Wie is a young golfer from Hawaii. Just six days before her sixteenth birthday, Wie announced that she was going to play professional golf. Wie has played as an amateur since she was a child. She spends most of her free time practicing. She practices three hours a day after school and seven to eight hours every weekend. Wie is on her way to becoming the richest female golfer in the world. She has already signed big deals with Nike and Sony. "I'm finally happy to say I'm a pro starting today," said Wie. "The first time I grabbed a golf club, I knew I'd do it for the rest of my life." Michelle Wie is definitely on her way.

Discussion

Discuss these questions in a small group.

1. Which do you prefer, watching sports on television or going to a game?
2. Who is your favorite athlete? Why?
3. What do you think is the most exciting sport? Why?
4. Do athletes in your country earn a lot of money?

Just for Fun

Complete the crossword puzzle with words from the unit.

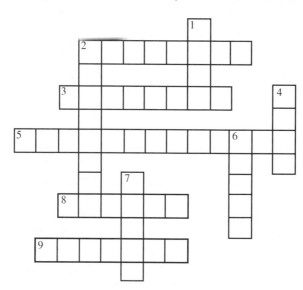

Across

2. *Sports Illustrated* is a sports _____.

3. You can become better at a sport if you _____ often.

5. having many cultural backgrounds

8. to ask someone to come to an event

9. someone who is very good at sports

Down

1. Ultimate players pass a _____ down a field.

2. a 26.2-mile race

4. the most popular sport in Scotland

6. The _____ of Ultimate are easy to learn.

7. Eldrick Woods's nickname is _____.

Sled Dog Racing

You will see a video about sled dog racing. What do you know about this sport? Have you ever watched a sled dog race?

A Study these words and phrase. Then watch the video.

familiar   prevents   sled

B Read these statements and then watch the video again. Circle the correct answer.

1. The first sled dog race was held in _____.
   a. Fairbanks, Alaska   **b.** Nome, Alaska

2. The Open North American Championships began in _____.
   a. 1906   **b.** 1946

3. The championship race lasts for _____.
   a. three days   **b.** three hours

4. The driver of the sled is called a _____.
   a. tracker   **b.** musher

5. The race track is _____ long.
   a. 20 miles   **b.** 20 kilometers

C Discuss these questions with a partner or in a small group.

1. Do you know of any other sports that involve animals? Have you ever watched or participated in any of them?
2. Do you think it is good to include animals in sports? Why or why not?

Reader's Journal   Think about the topics and ideas you have read about and discussed in this unit. Choose a topic from the list and write about it for ten to twenty minutes. Pick a topic from the following list, or choose one of your own.

- why you do or do not like sports
- your favorite sport
- your favorite sports team or athlete

Vocabulary Self-Test

Complete each sentence with the correct word or phrase.

A couple   invited   professional
        scored   trust

1. I _____ Rob to be careful with my car. I am going to let him use it this weekend.

2. I _____ ten people to my party.

3. Ali and Sara are the _____ who live next to us.

4. _____ soccer players get paid to play the sport.

5. Juan _____ the winning goal in the soccer game.

B attended   competitive   multicultural
        object   substitute

1. Elise is very _____. She gets upset if she doesn't win every game.

2. More than twenty-five people _____ the celebration.

3. Canada is a _____ country with many different kinds of people.

4. If you don't have sugar for your tea, use honey as a _____.

5. The _____ of the game is to score by kicking the ball into the goal.

C athlete   exchange   proud
        rules   took place

1. The graduation ceremony _____ last week.

2. Chin is good at a lot of sports. He is a great _____.

3. Let's _____ books. I want to read yours.

4. The _____ of this game are easy to learn.

5. Kyra's parents are very _____ of her. She gets excellent grades in school.

CITY SIGHTS

Most cities have interesting places to visit. In this unit, you will read about three interesting places in cities around the world.

Points to Ponder

Discuss these questions in a small group.

1. Look at the photo. Do you recognize this famous building? Are there any famous buildings in your city?

2. What is the most interesting place to visit in your city?

3. What is your favorite city? Why?

Istanbul's Grand Bazaar

Before You Read

A Discuss these questions with a partner.

1. Do you like to shop? Why or why not?
2. When you buy something, do you usually pay full price or do you try to pay less?
3. Find Istanbul, Turkey, on the map on page 00. Have you ever been to Istanbul?

B Study these words from the article. Write each word next to the correct definition.

bargain   crowded   explore
relax   tourists

1.	to rest
2.	to try to get a lower price on something you are buying
3.	to go around a place in order to learn more about it
4.	full of people
5.	people who visit a place for pleasure

ISTANBUL'S GRAND BAZAAR

1   There are many things to see and do if you visit Istanbul, Turkey. But Istanbul's Grand Bazaar is one place you must visit. It is the largest covered market in the world. It is an interesting place to **explore**, even if you don't like to shop.

An Exciting Place to Visit

2   Walking around the Grand Bazaar is exciting. It's like visiting a small town. There are more than 4,000 shops on sixty-five streets. The shops sell almost anything you want or need. You can buy Turkish carpets, jewelry, and clothes. You can also buy food and spices. The Grand Bazaar is always **crowded**. Every day, 250,000 people visit the Grand Bazaar. If you get hungry or need to **relax**, there are cafés, restaurants, and teahouses. There are also banks, a post office, and even a police station in the Grand Bazaar.

3   **Tourists** love to visit the Grand Bazaar, but it is not just for visitors. It is an important part of the lives of the people who live in Istanbul. They love the Grand Bazaar as much as the tourists do.

Tips for Tourists

4   Here are some suggestions for shopping at the Grand Bazaar. First, don't pay the first price the seller states. Always **bargain**. For example, if the price of a teapot is $25, you should offer to give the seller less. Say, "I'll give you $15." The seller will probably not take $15, but he may say, "I'll take $20." In Turkey, most people bargain before they buy something. The shopkeepers expect you to pay less than the price they are asking.

5   Second, don't buy the first thing you see. Remember that there is more of everything down the street. Look around before you buy. It's fun to explore the Grand Bazaar, but try not to get lost in the maze[1] of tiny streets.

6   Shopping may not be the best reason to go to Istanbul, but it is a very good reason to go there.

---

[1] **maze** –

After You Read

Comprehension Check

A Read these statements. If a statement is true, write *T* on the line. If it is false, write *F.*

_____ 1. Going to the Grand Bazaar is like going to a small town.

_____ 2. You cannot buy tea at the Grand Bazaar.

_____ 3. Only tourists go to the Grand Bazaar.

_____ 4. Shopkeepers expect you to pay more than the price they are asking.

_____ 5. Shopping is the only thing you can do at the Grand Bazaar.

B Circle the correct answer.

1. How many people visit the Grand Bazaar every day?
   a. 4,000
   b. 250,000

2. If you get hungry at the Grand Bazaar, you _____.
   a. have to leave to get something to eat
   b. can get something to eat there

3. How many shops are there in the Grand Bazaar?
   a. more than 4,000
   b. fewer than 4,000

4. What is at the Grand Bazaar, in addition to the shops?
   a. a movie theater and a school
   b. a police station and a post office

SKILL FOR SUCCESS

Identifying Facts and Opinions

When you read, it is important to understand the difference between facts and opinions. A **fact** is something that you can prove is true. An **opinion** is someone's idea.

There are twenty-five students in our class. (fact)

All of the students are very nice. (opinion)

C Decide if each statement is a fact or an opinion. Check the correct box.

	Fact	Opinion
1. Every day, 250,000 people visit the Grand Bazaar.		
2. Shopping is a very good reason to go to Istanbul.		
3. You can buy Turkish carpets, jewelry, and clothes at the bazaar.		
4. Walking around the Grand Bazaar is exciting.		
5. There are more than 4,000 shops on sixty-five streets.		
6. People who live in Istanbul love the Grand Bazaar as much as the tourists do.		

Vocabulary Practice

A Complete the paragraph with the words from the list.

bargain   crowded   explore   relax   tourists

If you go to Istanbul, you must visit the Grand Bazaar. You will probably find it very interesting to _____ the many shops
1.
and streets. Most people do. Every day, more than 250,000 people go to Istanbul's Grand Bazaar. It's a very _____ place. The people
2.
who live in Istanbul love the Grand Bazaar, and so do _____ who visit the city.
3.
At the Grand Bazaar, it is common to _____ with the
4.
shopkeeper before you buy something. Don't pay the first price the seller asks for. The seller will often take less money. When you get tired of bargaining and shopping, you can _____ at one of the
5.
many cafés.

B Circle the correct answer.

1. If a place is crowded, there are _____.
   a. only a few people there
   b. lots of people there

2. If you are a tourist in a country, you _____.
   a. are just visiting
   b. live there

3. When you bargain for something, you _____.
   a. agree to pay the seller's price
   b. offer to pay a lower price

4. If you explore a place, you _____.
   a. look around the place
   b. go home quickly

5. _____ is a common way to relax.
   a. Watching TV
   b. Going to work

✓**Understanding Word Forms**

C Read the sentences and decide if the underlined word is a noun or a verb. Check the correct box. Use your dictionary to help you.

	Noun	Verb
1. I like to visit new places.		
2. What did you do on your visit to New York?		
3. This is an exciting place to explore.		
4. Please place the box on the table.		
5. You should bargain before you buy something at the market.		
6. I got a great bargain on this ring.		
7. The shop closes in ten minutes.		
8. I like to shop in outdoor markets.		

Talk It Over

Discuss these questions as a class.

1. Would you like to shop in the Grand Bazaar? Why or why not?
2. Is there shopping area like the Grand Bazaar where you live? Do people there usually bargain when they shop?

Write an E-mail

Pretend you just visited the Grand Bazaar. Write about it in an e-mail to a friend. Try to use at least three new vocabulary words from this chapter. Compare e-mails with a partner.

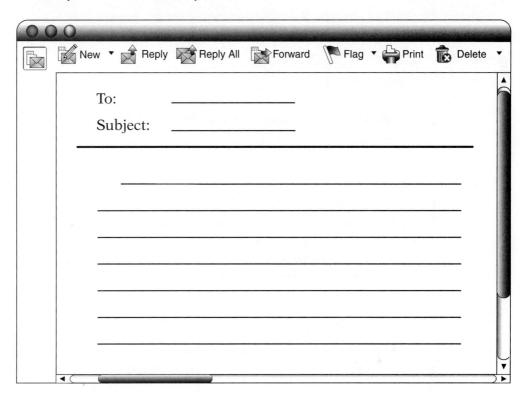

An Ice Hotel

Before You Read

A Discuss these questions with a partner.

1. How far north have you been? Have you ever been north of the Arctic Circle?
2. Do you like to stay in hotels? Do you think it would be fun to stay at a hotel made of ice? Why or why not?
3. What is the most famous hotel in your city? Why is it famous?

B Study these words and phrase from the article. Write each word or phrase next to the correct definition.

| employees | guests | make a reservation |
| melts | rebuild | |

1.	people who visit a home or stay at a hotel
2.	workers
3.	to arrange in advance to have a room (in a hotel) or a seat (on a plane or in a restaurant)
4.	becomes liquid
5.	to build again

C Follow these steps to make predictions about the article below.

1. Think about the title. Read the headings.
2. Look at the picture.
3. Check the ideas you think will be discussed in the article.

   ❑ **a.** how workers build the Icehotel

   ❑ **b.** what it's like to stay at the hotel

   ❑ **c.** things to do at the hotel

   ❑ **d.** problems with the hotel

   ❑ **e.** places to visit in Sweden

✓ **Skimming for the Main Idea**

D Skim the article one time. Circle the correct answer.

The article mainly discusses _____.

1. how to build an ice hotel
2. staying at an ice hotel
3. places to visit in Sweden

An Ice Hotel

1   Would you like to spend the night in a hotel made of ice? You can if you visit Jukkasjärvi, Sweden. There you will find the world's largest hotel made completely of ice and snow. The hotel is called Icehotel. It is very big. It's nearly 54,000 square feet (5,000 square meters). That's bigger than a soccer field.

Building the Hotel

2   Since the hotel is made of ice and snow, it **melts** every spring when the weather gets warmer. So every October, workers build a new hotel. The ice comes from the Torne River. The river is covered with about 3 feet (1 meter) of ice for most of the year. Workers use ice from the river to build the hotel. The walls, windows, doors, beds, chairs, and tables are all made of ice. After the building is finished, the hotel has about eighty-five rooms. The first **guests** come in December.

Keeping Warm in the Hotel

3   What is it like to stay in the hotel? The hotel is about 120 miles (200 kilometers) north of the Arctic Circle, so the temperature outside — and inside — is cold. Inside the hotel, the temperature is about 23 degrees Fahrenheit (-5 degrees Celsius). Hotel

employees suggest that guests dress warmly. It's a good idea to wear at least three layers of clothing. And at night, guests sleep in very warm sleeping bags. The cold doesn't stop people from coming to the hotel. Lots of people come every year. Last year, more than 14,000 guests stayed at the hotel! So if you plan to visit the Icehotel, be sure to **make a reservation**.

Things to Do at the Icehotel

4   There are lots of things to do at the Icehotel. There is an excellent restaurant that serves wonderful food on plates made of ice. Guests can watch movies in an ice theater or look at the paintings and sculptures at the ice art show. The Icehotel also has a beautiful ice church. Couples come from all over the world to get married there.

A Different Hotel Every Year

5   By late April, the Icehotel gets warm and begins to melt. Soon it becomes a water hotel. Every year workers have to **rebuild** the Icehotel, so every year it is different. Just like no two snowflakes are the same, no two Icehotels are the same.

After You Read

Comprehension Check

A Read these statements. If a statement is true, write *T* on the line. If it is false, write *F*.

_____ **1.** The Icehotel is the world's biggest hotel made of ice and snow.

_____ **2.** The beds are made of wood.

_____ **3.** Guests at the hotel should dress warmly.

_____ **4.** The Icehotel looks the same every year.

_____ **5.** The Icehotel has a church and a movie theater.

B Scan the article to match each question with the correct answer.

Question   **Answer**

_____ 1. Where is the Icehotel?   a. 14,000

_____ 2. How big is the Icehotel?   b. 23 degrees Fahrenheit

_____ 3. How many guests stayed   c. in October
         at the Icehotel last year?
                                                             d. nearly 54,000 square feet
_____ 4. What is the temperature
         inside the Icehotel?   e. in Jukkasjärvi, Sweden

_____ 5. When do workers begin   f. by late April
         building each new Icehotel?

_____ 6. When does the Icehotel
         begin to melt?

Vocabulary Practice

A Complete each sentence with the correct word(s) or phrase.

employees	guests	make a reservation
melts	rebuild	

1. The first _____ come to the Icehotel in December.

2. The hotel's _____ give suggestions about how to stay warm.

3. In the spring, the Icehotel _____. So, every year workers have to _____ the Icehotel.

4. You should _____ if you want to stay at the Icehotel.

B Circle the correct answer.

1. An <u>employee</u> at the Icehotel is someone who _____.
   a. visits the Icehotel
   b. works at the Icehotel

2. If you <u>make a reservation</u> at a restaurant, you _____.
   a. don't want to go there
   b. plan to go there

3. A <u>guest</u> at a hotel _____.
   a. pays to stay there
   b. serves food there

4. When workers <u>rebuild</u> the Icehotel, they _____.

    a. build it again

    b. stay there again

5. When ice <u>melts</u>, it becomes _____.

    a. colder

    b. water

SKILL FOR SUCCESS

Understanding Word Parts: The Prefix *re-*
The prefix *re-* is common in English. *Re-* is usually added to a word to mean *to do again.* For example, the word *rebuild* from the article means *build again.*

C Complete each sentence with the correct word. Use your dictionary to help you.

rearrange   recycle   reread   resend

1. I did not understand the paragraph. I need to _____ it.

2. I did not get your e-mail. Please _____ it to me.

3. I want to change the way this room looks. I think I will

    _____ the furniture.

4. It is important to _____ old newspapers, bottles, and cans.

Read E-mails

Read the four e-mails that Emma wrote to her friend while visiting Costa Rica. Then match each e-mail with the photo on page 168 that she took that day.

1. _____

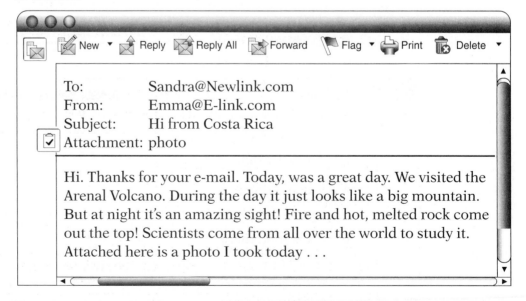

To: Sandra@Newlink.com
From: Emma@E-link.com
Subject: Hi from Costa Rica
Attachment: photo

Hi. Thanks for your e-mail. Today, was a great day. We visited the Arenal Volcano. During the day it just looks like a big mountain. But at night it's an amazing sight! Fire and hot, melted rock come out the top! Scientists come from all over the world to study it. Attached here is a photo I took today . . .

2. _____

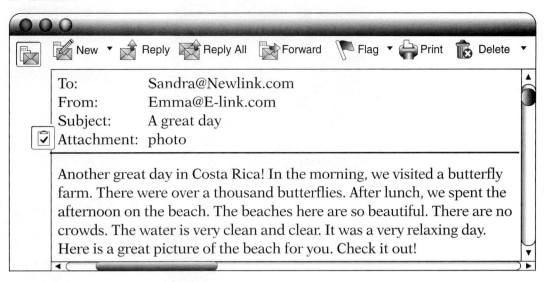

To: Sandra@Newlink.com
From: Emma@E-link.com
Subject: A great day
Attachment: photo

Another great day in Costa Rica! In the morning, we visited a butterfly farm. There were over a thousand butterflies. After lunch, we spent the afternoon on the beach. The beaches here are so beautiful. There are no crowds. The water is very clean and clear. It was a very relaxing day. Here is a great picture of the beach for you. Check it out!

3. _____

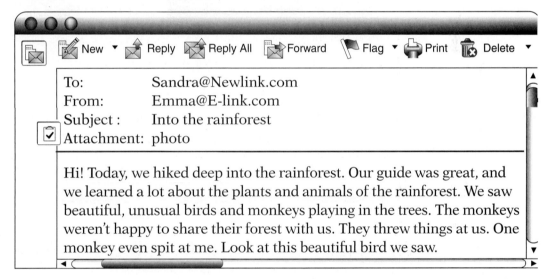

To: Sandra@Newlink.com
From: Emma@E-link.com
Subject : Into the rainforest
Attachment: photo

Hi! Today, we hiked deep into the rainforest. Our guide was great, and we learned a lot about the plants and animals of the rainforest. We saw beautiful, unusual birds and monkeys playing in the trees. The monkeys weren't happy to share their forest with us. They threw things at us. One monkey even spit at me. Look at this beautiful bird we saw.

4. _____

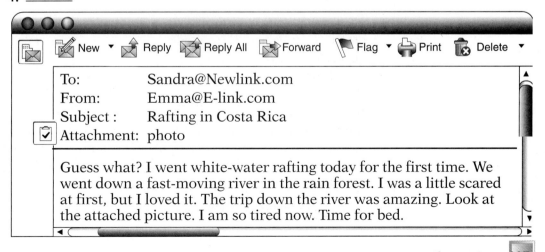

To: Sandra@Newlink.com
From: Emma@E-link.com
Subject : Rafting in Costa Rica
Attachment: photo

Guess what? I went white-water rafting today for the first time. We went down a fast-moving river in the rain forest. I was a little scared at first, but I loved it. The trip down the river was amazing. Look at the attached picture. I am so tired now. Time for bed.

a.

b.

c.

d.

Write an E-mail

Pretend you are staying at the Icehotel. Write about it in an e-mail to a friend. Try to use at least three new vocabulary words from this chapter. Compare e-mails with a partner.

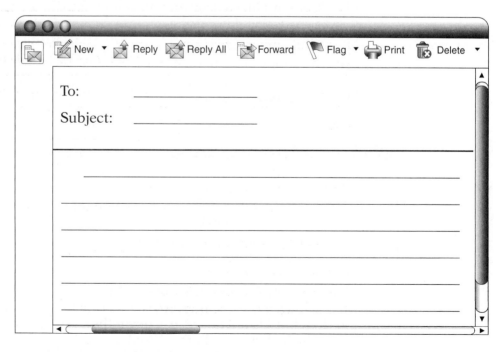

Sister Cities Exchange Gifts

Before You Read

A Discuss these questions with a partner.

1. Have you ever been to a teahouse? Is there a teahouse in your city?
2. Have you ever been to a cyber café? Is there a cyber café in your city?
3. Have you heard of a group called Sister Cities International? Does your city have a Sister City?

B Study these words from the article. Write each word next to the correct definition.

capital   citizens   gorgeous   international   socialize

1.	the people who live in a city or country
2.	the city where a country's main government is
3.	to spend time with people in a friendly way
4.	for, from, or with many countries
5.	very beautiful

✓ **Skimming for the Main Idea**

C Skim the article one time. Circle the correct answer.

The article mainly discusses _____.

1. two cities that shared gifts
2. cyber cafés around the world
3. meeting friends at teahouses

Sister Cities Exchange Gifts

1   Dushanbe is the **capital** of the Republic of Tajikistan in Central Asia. The U.S. city of Boulder, Colorado, is on the other side of the world. Dushanbe and Boulder are Sister Cities. They belong to an organization called Sister Cities **International**. The organization supports international friendship, peace, and understanding.

2   In 1989, the people of Dushanbe gave a beautiful teahouse to the **citizens** of Boulder. The teahouse is truly beautiful to see. Inside, the walls are covered with colorful handmade tiles. There are also a fountain and many pieces of art. Visitors can enjoy the beauty inside the teahouse, or they can sit outside and admire the **gorgeous** flower garden.

3   In Tajikistan, teahouses are places where people meet to drink tea, eat, talk, and play chess. The teahouse in Boulder is also a place where people meet to **socialize**, eat, and drink tea. More than 100,000 people visit the teahouse each year. The teahouse serves food from many cultures. It also serves teas from around the world.

Dushanbe gave Boulder this beautiful traditional teahouse.

4   Now, Boulder's **citizens** want to give a gift to the people of Dushanbe. They are going to give them a cyber café. A cyber café is a café or

coffeehouse that has computers for its customers to use. Cyber cafés are popular in many cities around the world. Now, Dushanbe will have a cyber café, too. The cyber café in Dushanbe will have eighteen computers. It will also have a restaurant and a library. It will be a great place for people to meet, talk, e-mail friends, eat, and have fun. The people of Boulder hope the citizens of Dushanbe will enjoy the cyber café as much as the teahouse in Boulder is enjoyed.

5 The Dushanbe and Boulder Sister Cities' relationship shows how people can connect with one another around the world. It is a wonderful example of international friendship, peace, and understanding.

After You Read

Comprehension Check

A Circle the correct answer.

1. Where is Dushanbe?
   a. in Colorado
   b. in the Republic of Tajikistan
   c. in South Asia

2. What did the people of Dushanbe give to Boulder?
   a. a cyber café
   b. a teahouse
   c. eighteen computers

3. What is Boulder giving to Dushanbe?
   a. a cyber café
   b. pieces of art
   c. a rose garden

4. What does Sister Cities International do?
   a. build restaurants and libraries around the world
   b. support international friendship and understanding
   c. create beautiful art

✓ Identifying Facts and Opinions

B Decide if each statement is a fact or an opinion. Check the correct box.

	Fact	Opinion
1. Dushanbe is the capital of the Republic of Tajikistan.		
2. A cyber café is a café with computers for its customers to use.		
3. More than 100,000 people visit the teahouse each year.		
4. Dushanbe and Boulder's relationship is a wonderful example of international friendship		
5. The cyber café in Dushanbe will have eighteen computers.		
6. The cyber café will be a great place for people to talk, e-mail friends, eat, and have fun.		

Vocabulary Practice

A Complete each sentence with the correct word.

capital   citizens   gorgeous
international   socialize

1. The _____ of Dushanbe gave Boulder a wonderful gift.

2. There is a _____ flower garden outside of the teahouse.

3. The Boulder-Dushanbe Sister Cities' relationship is an example of _____ friendship, peace, and understanding.

4. The _____ of Tajikistan is Dushanbe.

5. Teahouses and cyber cafés are great places to _____.

B Ask and answer these questions with a partner.

1. Where do you usually go to socialize with friends?
2. What country are you a citizen of?
3. What is the capital of your native country?
4. What is the most gorgeous garden you have ever seen?
5. Do you think Sister Cities can help create international friendship? How?

Understanding Word Parts: The Suffix *-ful*

The suffix *-ful* is added to a word to mean *full of*. For example, the word *colorful* from the reading means *full of color*.

C Add the suffix *-ful* to each word. Then write a sentence using the new word. Use your dictionary to help you. Compare sentences with a partner.

1. care_____

_____

2. thank_____

_____

3. wonder_____

_____

4. use_____

_____

5. power_____

_____

Talk It Over

Discuss these questions as a class.

1. The article says that Sister City relationships help build international friendship, peace, and understanding. Do you agree or disagree? Why?
2. What can we all do to spread friendship, understanding, and peace throughout the world?
3. Do you think teahouses and cyber cafés are good places to socialize? Why or why not?

Make a Poster

In a small group, discuss ways people can build international friendships. Make a poster that explains at least three ways. Show your poster to the rest of the class.

Discussion

Discuss these questions in a small group.

1. What is the most popular place to visit in your city?
2. What suggestions do you have for tourists visiting your city?
3. Which place described in this unit would you most like to visit? Why?

Just for Fun

You have been traveling around the world, and now you want to go home. Find your way home through the maze.

abc NEWS

Video Activity

Icehotel

This video is about the Icehotel. What do you remember about the Icehotel from the second article in this unit? What else do you hope to learn about it?

A Study these words and phrases. Then watch the video.

comfortable   entertainment   igloo

B Watch the video again. Write four words or phrases that describe the Icehotel.

_____   _____   _____

_____

C Discuss these questions with a partner or in a small group.

If you could invent an unusual type of hotel, what would it be like? Where would you build it? What would be special about it?

Reader's Journal Think about the topics and ideas you have read about and discussed in this unit. Choose a topic from the list and write about it for ten to twenty minutes. Pick a topic from the following list, or choose one of your own.

• your favorite city
• why Sister Cities are a good idea
• an interesting place you have visited

Vocabulary Self-Test

Complete each sentence with the correct word or phrase.

A   capital   crowded   employee
        guests   socialize

1. When you work for a company, you are an _____.

2. Cairo is the _____ of Egypt.

3. Shamsul doesn't like to _____ with people he doesn't know.

4. The bus was very _____. There were not enough seats for everyone.

5. The hotel has rooms for 100 _____.

B   citizens   explore   gorgeous
        international   make a reservation

1. Let's eat at that new restaurant. I'll _____ for 8 P.M.

2. Ahmed is going to _____ southern Spain during his vacation.

3. The _____ of the country were proud to host the Olympic Games.

4. People from many countries will come to the meeting this year. It will be an _____ meeting.

5. Yesterday was warm, sunny, and _____.

C   bargain   melt   rebuild
        relax   tourists

1. Sometimes it's hard to _____ after working all day.

2. The Jensens' house was badly burned in the fire, but they will _____ it.

3. Paris a very popular city with _____.

4. Ice will _____ if the temperature goes above 32 degrees Fahrenheit (0 degrees Celsius).

5. I tried to _____ with the owner of the store. I wanted him to lower the price.

Vocabulary Self-Tests Answer Key

Unit 1
(page 20)

A 1. honest
   2. goal
   3. popular
   4. vacation
   5. choose
   6. twice

B 1. intelligent
   2. celebrate
   3. favorite
   4. disease
   5. exciting

C 1. customs
   2. special
   3. hobby
   4. similar
   5. headache

Unit 2
(page 44)

A 1. cookbook
   2. seafood
   3. neighborhood
   4. smelly
   5. fired

B 1. invented
   2. noisy
   3. dessert
   4. recipe
   5. huge

C 1. note
   2. handmade
   3. famous
   4. menu
   5. unusual

Unit 3
(page 65)

A 1. control
   2. Technology
   3. lose touch with
   4. educational
   5. message

B 1. useful
   2. inexpensive
   3. make a habit of
   4. hear from
   5. graduation

C 1. free
   2. lonely
   3. make a commitment
   4. figure out
   5. put on

Unit 4
(page 89)

A 1. disappoint
   2. for a living
   3. successful
   4. adventure
   5. fashionable
   6. jewelry

B 1. report
   2. forecasted
   3. earns
   4. occupation
   5. boss
   6. draw

C 1. career
   2. challenge
   3. continued
   4. take a break
   5. interviewed

Unit 5
(page 109)

A 1. wise
   2. disappear
   3. ceremony
   4. kindergarten
   5. fluent

B 1. accomplishment
   2. weird
   3. expressed
   4. community
   5. simple

C 1. enormous
   2. equal
   3. foolish
   4. contest
   5. honor

Unit 6
(page 132)

A 1. vote
   2. diet
   3. command
   4. starve
   5. journey

B 1. exhausted
   2. glad
   3. trains
   4. rare
   5. pick up

C 1. disability
   2. turn on
   3. curious
   4. thin
   5. habitat

Unit 7
(page 154)

A 1. trust
    2. invited
    3. couple
    4. Professional
    5. scored

B 1. competitive
    2. attended
    3. multicultural
    4. substitute
    5. object

C 1. took place
    2. athlete
    3. exchange
    4. rules
    5. proud

Unit 8
(page 176)

A 1. employee
    2. capital
    3. socialize
    4. crowded
    5. guests

B 1. make a reservation
    2. explore
    3. citizens
    4. international
    5. gorgeous

C 1. relax
    2. rebuild
    3. tourists
    4. melt
    5. bargain

Glossary

A

accomplishments (104): things that you have done well or with success

adventure (74): an exciting activity

athletes (139): people who are good at sports

attended (134): went to an event

B

bargain (156): to try to get a lower price on something you are buying

boss (74): a person who tells other people what work to do

C

capital (169): the city where a country's main government is

career (82): a job that you know a lot about and do for a long time

celebrated (2): had a special meal or party for an important event

ceremonies (98): important events that celebrate something

challenge (74): something difficult that tests your ability

choose (7): to decide which thing you want

citizens (169): the people who live in a city or country

commands (112): orders

community (104): all the people living in a place

competitive (145): wanting to win or be the best

contests (98): competitions for a prize

continued (82): kept doing without stopping

control (58): to make something do what you want

cookbook (23): a book that tells you how to make and cook foods

couple (134): two people who are married or have a romantic relationship

crowded (156): full of people

curious (123): wanting learn or try new things

customs (7): ways of behaving that have been done for a long time

D

daughters (2): female children

dessert (23): a sweet food that you eat after a meal

diet (117): the food that you eat

disabilities (112): diseases or injuries that make it hard for people to do the things that other people do

disappears (92): stops existing or being

disappoint (82): to make someone unhappy because something is not as good as he or she wanted it to be

disease (2): a sickness

draw (82): to make a picture using a pencil or pen

E

earn (74): to get something, usually money, for doing work

educational (47): helping you to learn

employees (162): workers

enormous (92): very big

equal (92): having the same amount or level

exchanged (134): gave something to someone and received something from him or her

exciting (2): making you feel very happy or interested

exhausted (123): very tired

explore (156): to go around a place in order to learn more about it

express (92): to say or do something to let people know what you think or how you feel

F

famous (29): known and liked by many people

fashionable (68): popular at a particular time; in style

favorite (13): best liked

figured out (58): understood something after thinking about it

fired (34): ordered to leave a job

fluent (104): able to speak or write a language very well

foolish (98): not intelligent

for a living (82): in order to earn money

forecast (68): to say what you think will happen in the future

free (47): not costing any money

G

glad (123): happy

goal (2): something you want to do or make happen

gorgeous (169): very beautiful

graduation (47): the time when you complete school and receive a diploma or degree

guests (162): people who visit a home or stay at a hotel

H

habitat (117): the place where a plant or animal lives

handmade (34): made by a person, not by a machine

headache (13): a pain you feel inside your head

hear from (53): to get news or information from someone

hobby (13): an activity that you enjoy doing

honest (7): truthful; not likely to lie or steal

honor (98): to show that you have good feelings for someone or something

huge (29): very big

I

inexpensive (47): low in price

intelligent (7): smart; able to learn and understand things easily

international (169): for, from, or with many countries

interviews (68): asks someone questions

invented (34): made something for the first time

invite (134): to ask someone to come to an event

J

jewelry (68): things such as rings and necklaces that you wear on your body

journey (123): a long trip

K

kindergarten (104): the first year of school, for children age five

L

lonely (53): unhappy because you are not with other people

lose touch with (53): to stop having regular communication with someone

M

make a commitment (53): to promise to do something

make a habit of (53): to do something often and regularly

make a reservation (162): to arrange in advance to have a room (in a hotel) or a seat (on a plane or in a restaurant)

melts (162): becomes liquid

menu (23): a list of the food served in a restaurant

message (47): a small amount of information that you send to someone

multicultural (139): having many cultural backgrounds

N

neighborhood (34): a small area of town where people live

noisy (29): making or having loud sounds

note (34): a short piece of writing

O

object (145): purpose

occupation (68): a person's job

P

picks up (112): holds and lifts something

popular (7): liked by many people

professional (139): doing an activity for money

proud (139): feeling happy about something good that you do or have

put on (58): to cover part of your body with clothes, shoes, etc.

R

rare (117): not happening or seen very often

rebuild (162): to build again

recipes (23): instructions that tell you how to cook things

relax (156): to rest

report (68): a piece of writing that gives people information

rules (145): things that tell you what you can and cannot do

S

score (145): to win a point in a game

seafood (29): ocean animals that can be eaten

similar (13): almost the same

simple (92): easy to learn or understand

smelly (29): having a bad smell

socialize (169): to spend time with people in a friendly way

special (2): better or more important than most things

starve (117): to die or become sick because you do not have enough to eat

substitute (139): something that you can exchange for another thing

success (74): having a good result; popular

T

take a break (74): to stop doing something for a short time

technology (58): knowledge, machines, and methods used in science and industry

thin (123): not fat

took place (134): happened

tourists (156): people who visit a place for pleasure

trains (112): teaches

trust (145): to believe someone is honest or good

turn on (112): to make something start working

twice (13): two times

U

unusual (23): not common

useful (58): helping you do something

V

vacation (13): time away from work or school when you can travel or rest

vote (117): to express your choice, especially by marking a paper or by raising your hand

W

weird (104): strange and unusual

wise (98): having great knowledge and understanding

Map of the United States

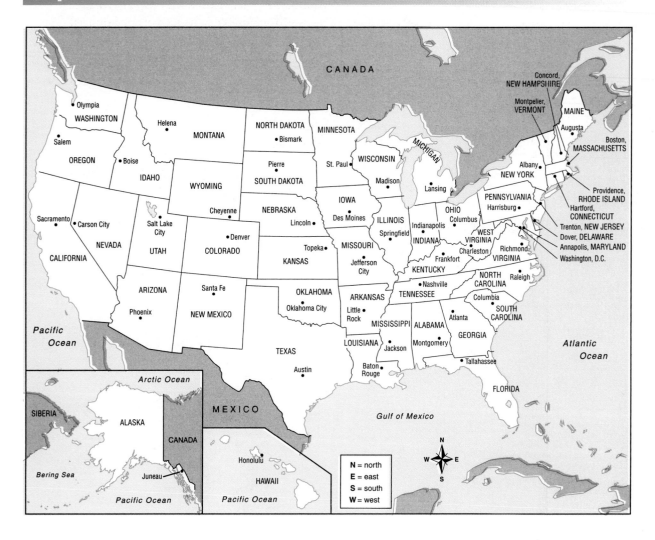

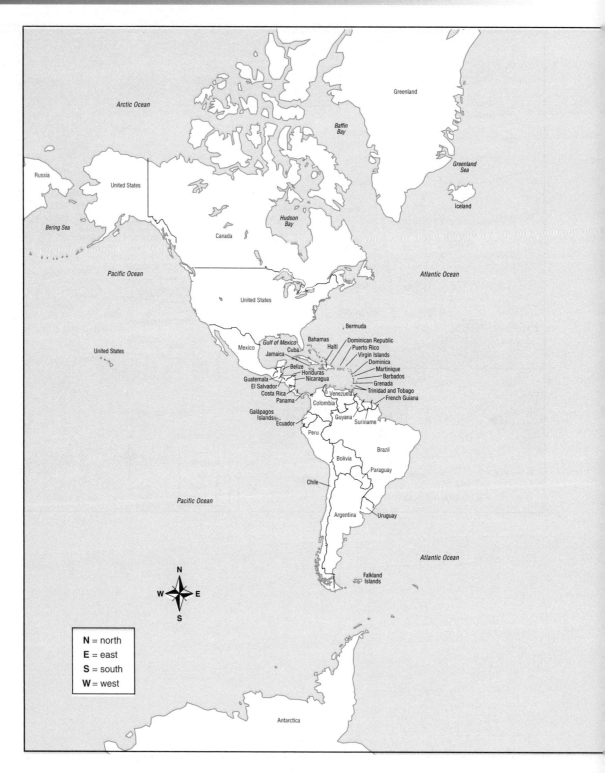

N = north
E = east
S = south
W = west

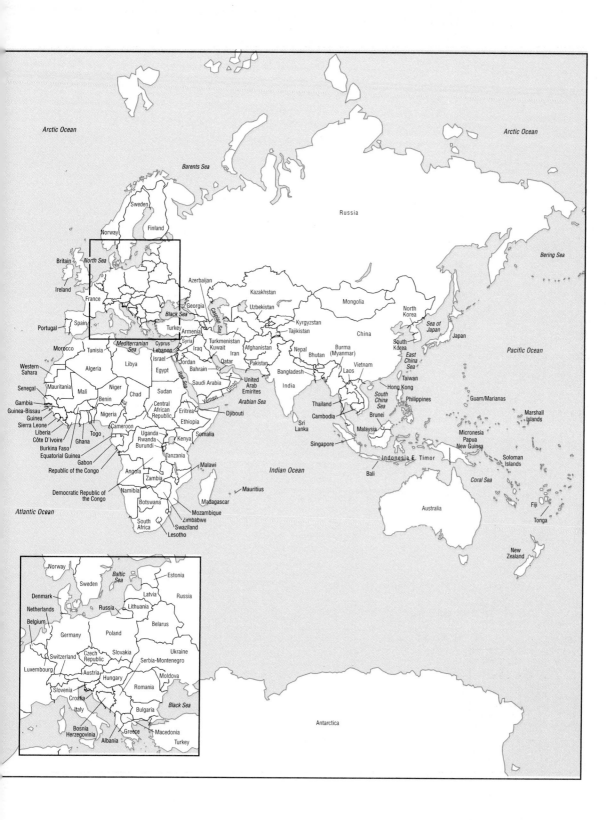

Arctic Ocean

Arctic Ocean

Barents Sea

Bering Sea

Sweden

Norway

Finland

Russia

Britain

North Sea

Ireland

France

Azerbaijan

Kazakhstan

Mongolia

North
Korea

Sea of
Japan

Japan

Pacific Ocean

Portugal

Spain

Black Sea

Georgia

Uzbekistan

Kyrgyzstan

South
Korea

Turkey

Armenia

Tajikistan

China

Morocco

Tunisia

Mediterranean
Sea

Cyprus
Lebanon

Syria

Iraq

Turkmenistan
Kuwait

Afghanistan

Nepal

Bhutan

Burma
(Myanmar)

Vietnam

East
China
Sea

Taiwan

Western
Sahara

Algeria

Libya

Israel
Jordan

Bahrain

Iran

Qatar

Pakistan

India

Bangladesh

Laos

Hong Kong

Senegal

Mauritania

Mali

Niger

Chad

Egypt

Saudi Arabia

United
Arab
Emirites

South
China
Sea

Philippines

Guam/Marianas

Gambia

Benin

Sudan

Yemen

Oman

Arabian Sea

Thailand

Cambodia

Brunei

Marshall
Islands

Guinea-Bissau

Nigeria

Central
African
Republic

Eritrea

Djibouti

Sri
Lanka

Malaysia

Micronesia

Guinea

Cameroon

Ethiopia

Singapore

Papua
New Guinea

Sierra Leone

Liberia

Togo

Uganda

Somalia

Soloman
Islands

Côte D'Ivoire

Ghana

Rwanda

Kenya

Indonesia E. Timor

Burkina Faso

Burundi

Tanzania

Bali

Fiji

Equatorial Guinea

Gabon

Malawi

Indian Ocean

Coral Sea

Tonga

Republic of the Congo

Angola

Zambia

Mauritius

Democratic Republic of
the Congo

Namibia

Botswana

Madagascar

Australia

Atlantic Ocean

South
Africa

Zimbabwe

Mozambique

Swaziland

Lesotho

New
Zealand

Norway

Baltic
Sea

Estonia

Sweden

Latvia

Russia

Denmark

Russia

Lithuania

Netherlands

Belarus

Belgium

Germany

Poland

Switzerland

Czech
Republic

Slovakia

Ukraine

Luxembourg

Austria

Serbia-Montenegro

Hungary

Moldova

Slovenia

Croatia

Romania

Italy

Bulgaria

Black Sea

Bosnia
Herzegovinia

Greece

Macedonia

Albania

Turkey

Antarctica

Map of the World   **185**

Unit 1   All In the Family

_____

_____

_____

_____

_____

_____

_____

Unit 2   Let's Eat

_____

_____

_____

_____

_____

_____

_____

_____

Unit 3 Keeping In Touch

_____

_____

_____

_____

_____

_____

_____

Unit 4 The Work World

_____

_____

_____

_____

_____

_____

_____

_____

Unit 5 Language and Life

_____

_____

_____

_____

_____

_____

_____

Unit 6 Animal Tales

_____

_____

_____

_____

_____

_____

_____

Unit 7 Sports Stories

_____

_____

_____

_____

_____

_____

_____

Unit 8 City Sights

_____

_____

_____

_____

_____

_____

_____